THIS DAY IN HISTORY

GREAT
LEADERS

AURA

This edition published in 2019 by Baker and Taylor (UK)
Ltd, Bicester, Oxfordshire, OX26 4ST

ISBN 978-0-85762-948-7

Conceived, designed and produced by The Bright Press,
an imprint of The Quarto Group
The Old Brewery
6 Blundell Street
London N7 9BH
United Kingdom
T (0) 20 7700 6700 F (0) 20 7700 8066
www.QuartoKnows.com

Manufactured in Singapore

10 9 8 7 6 5 4 3 2 1

Publisher: Mark Searle
Creative Director: James Evans
Managing Editor: Jacqui Sayers
Editor: Abbie Sharman
Designer: JC Lanaway
Cover and layout design: Greg Stalley

Cover Image Credits (top to bottom)
Renata Sedmakova/ Shutterstock, Everett Historical/
Shutterstock, Stockphotocorner/ Shutterstock,
Nigel Jarvis/ Shutterstock

365

LANDMARK EVENTS

THIS DAY IN HISTORY

GREAT LEADERS

SARAH HERMAN

AURA

Contents

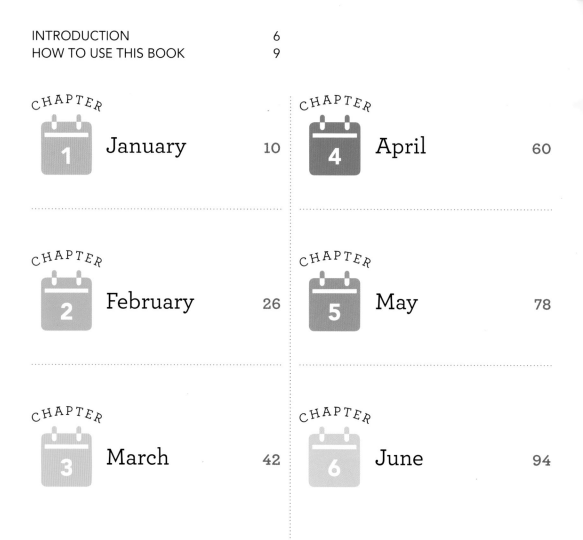

> " Some are born great, some
> achieve greatness, and some
> have greatness thrust upon 'em. "
>
> MALVOLIO IN *TWELFTH NIGHT* BY WILLIAM SHAKESPEARE

Introduction

At a time when great leaders seem few and far between, it is comforting to look back at the brilliant women and men who shaped the world we live in through outstanding governance, military might or determined domination. From the constitution-defining decisions of Abraham Lincoln to the nation-stirring speeches of Winston Churchill, this book travels through time to the moments from history that founded empires, made monarchies, ended wars, galvanised movements and spread religions across the globe, all thanks to the people in charge.

> **Stand with anybody that stands right, stand with him while he is right and part with him when he goes wrong.**
> ABRAHAM LINCOLN

For the sake of this book, a 'Great Leader' is someone who effected important change in their lifetime, in most cases for the good. There are both literal leaders – monarchs, heads of state and military generals, for example – and those who have led movements and organisations to prodigious acclaim. Some of the people included are iconic, their names known around the world, and some less so, but their place in the history books is no less significant.

▶ Winston Churchill waves to his followers.

Though some moments will resonate with most readers, seared in a collective memory, others might be new to you. Martin Luther King Jr's 'I have a dream' speech of 1963 is as unforgettable as the day Nelson Mandela was freed from prison after 27 years on 11th February, 1990. The fearless victory of Sitting Bull and Crazy Horse at the Battle of Little Bighorn in June 1876 made an indelible mark on history, as did suffragette Emmeline Pankhurst's speech inciting women to rebellion at the Albert Hall in October 1912.

> **“ I have a dream that... one day right there in Alabama, little black boys and black girls will be able to join hands with little white boys and white girls as sisters and brothers. ”**
>
> MARTIN LUTHER KING JR, 1963

In this book you will read about the heroism of naval commanders, Mongolian warlords, Roman emperors and civil rights activists. Learn about the women who fought for equality and the men who conquered new lands; the queens who transformed nations and the politicians who changed laws; the powerful who wielded their power wisely and those who used their power for evil as well as the powerless who found a voice.

How to use this book

This is a book you can enjoy today, tomorrow and the whole year round. For each day of the year you will find at least one corresponding entry that tells you about something that happened on that date in history, relating to a famous leader. It might be their birthday, the day they died or something significant that happened in their lifetime – from victorious battles and milestone marches to election wins and stirring speeches.

You will notice that some dates have a longer entry with a bit more detail to enjoy, while others come with a bonus 'also on this day' section, when one key event just wasn't enough. Most months have a 'week to view' section, including small snippets of key leadership moments from that week throughout history. We recommend enjoying the book by reading one entry each day to build up an interesting picture of leadership throughout the year, giving you a thought-provoking factoid to share on the very day that it happened.

Inspire your colleagues with a regular dose of how the greats got things done; impress your friends with facts galore; and take a moment each day to remember the trailblazers who took charge and changed the world.

Military commander

Monarch, Emperor, Chief

Politician, political movement or event

Religious leader, event or religion

Activist, social movement or organisation

Science, technology, medicine and philosophy

Legal

Industrialist, Philanthropist, Author

Pioneer, Explorer

You will also spot the icons above that appear throughout the book. These let you see, at a glance, to what type of person the entry relates: whether it is a monarch, political leader, religious leader, military commander, or head of a social movement or organisation. They are also colour-coded for your convenience.

CHAPTER

1

January

QUEEN VICTORIA IS PROCLAIMED EMPRESS OF INDIA

Princess Victoria was a minor royal when she was born but became Queen of the United Kingdom after the death of her uncle King William IV. At 18 she ascended to the throne and reigned for 63 years (1837–1901) during a time of imperial expansion and British dominance on the world stage, in which she took great interest. Though Victoria never travelled as far as India, British Prime Minister Benjamin Disraeli pushed the unpopular Royal Titles Bill through Parliament to issue her with this new title, in an effort to strengthen the ties between the two countries. Lord Lytton, viceroy of India, held celebrations in Delhi to mark the occasion.

The Royal Titles Bill was pushed through Parliament to help strengthen the ties between the United Kingdom and India.

▲ A large crowd gathered to see Queen Victoria proclaimed Empress of India.

JANUARY

2

1960

SENATOR JOHN F. KENNEDY ANNOUNCES HIS CANDIDACY

In a packed US Senate Caucus Room (now known as the Kennedy Caucus Room) of the Russell Senate Office Building, Washington, DC, the senator from Massachusetts announced his candidacy for the presidency of the United States. After seven years in the Senate, Kennedy had made a name for himself as a liberal and idealistic Democrat, and he had almost become the vice-presidential nominee in 1956. He told the press:

> **I have developed an image of America as fulfilling a noble and historic role as the defender of freedom in a time of maximum peril – and of the American people as confident, courageous and persevering. It is with this image that I begin this campaign.**

JANUARY

3

1521

MARTIN LUTHER IS EXCOMMUNICATED

Martin Luther was an Augustinian friar who taught theology at the University of Erfurt, Germany, in the 16th century. His excommunication by Pope Leo X came after he published a work known as the *95 Theses* condemning the Roman Catholic Church for selling 'indulgences' – documents absolving the bearer from sin. Luther believed that Christians would be saved through their faith and not through these corrupt practices. Europe's now well-established printing press allowed Luther's writings to spread quickly across the continent, where he gained lots of support. His followers named themselves Lutherans.

Luther was summoned to appear at a meeting of the Holy Roman Empire in the now-German city of Worms – the Diet (assembly) of Worms – where he famously refused to recant his writings. Emperor Charles V branded him an outlaw and a heretic as a result.

JANUARY
4
2007

FIRST FEMALE SPEAKER FOR THE US HOUSE OF REPRESENTATIVES

When the 110th United States Congress convened, the Democratic Party had gained 31 seats in the mid-term elections and reclaimed control of the chamber for the first time in over a decade. Nancy Pelosi, a longstanding representative from California, had been the minority leader for four years when she was elected speaker. She was the first woman to lead a party in Congress, and as speaker (second in the line of presidential succession after the vice president) she reached the highest position of power so far achieved by a woman in the United States. She held the post until 2011, and then reassumed it in 2019.

During her first speech as speaker she said:

> " For our daughters and granddaughters, today, we have broken the marble ceiling. For our daughters and our granddaughters, the sky is the limit, anything is possible for them. "

JANUARY
5
1914

HENRY FORD DOUBLES HIS WORKERS' PAY

> " Figure out how much more we can give our men. "
> HENRY FORD

That's what the industrialist and founder of Ford Motors, Henry Ford, said when he walked into a 1914 wage-scale meeting. At the time, automakers were getting $2.34 for a nine-hour day, but Ford recognised the importance of investing in his workers and alleviating the monotony of the production line. He cut the working day to eight hours and more than doubled the minimum day wage to $5. His actions shocked the industry, but Ford stood firm, believing that well-paid workers would become potential customers. And he was right – by 1920 Ford was selling one million cars a year.

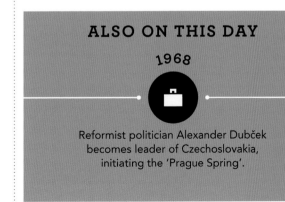

ALSO ON THIS DAY
1968

Reformist politician Alexander Dubček becomes leader of Czechoslovakia, initiating the 'Prague Spring'.

JANUARY

6

1929

MOTHER TERESA ARRIVES IN CALCUTTA TO BEGIN HER WORK AMONG INDIA'S POOREST

Albanian nun Agnes Gonxha Bojaxhiu, more commonly known as Mother Teresa, was just 18 when she arrived in Calcutta (now called Kolkata) for the first time. She had travelled from Ireland, where she had been a postulant at the Loreto Convent in Rathfarnam. Having long been enchanted by stories of Catholics working in the Far East, she joined the Loreto novitiate in Darjeeling, worked in Kolkata's St Mary's high school and made her final profession on 24th May, 1937. It would be another nine years before she received her 'call within a call' to serve the poorest people living on the city's streets – a calling that would make her a household name around the world.

▼ Mother Teresa visits the sick in a death chamber in Kolkata, India.

JANUARY

7

1698

RUSSIAN TSAR PETER THE GREAT SETS SAIL FOR ENGLAND

William III, King of England, Ireland and Scotland, invited the Russian ruler to cross the English Channel from the Dutch Republic (of which William was also *stadtholder*, or chief magistrate). The 25-year-old tsar, travelling under the alias 'Peter Mikhailov', had left Russia behind the year before to experience the culture and advancements of Western Europe. The aim of his incognito trip was to bring back knowledge and ideas to transform his home country into a modern nation. While in England, he studied the English military arsenal, toured historical sites and explored the country's rich artistic culture. He returned home a few months later, greatly impressed by the open-debate style of English politics and by the island nation's shipbuilding prowess. He had soon established a shipbuilding program of his own and expanded the Russian navy. His exploits would lead to his becoming one of Russia's most renowned rulers.

> Peter the Great established a shipbuilding program of his own and expanded the Russian navy.

JANUARY

8

1790

GEORGE WASHINGTON'S FIRST ANNUAL MESSAGE TO CONGRESS

President Washington's first Annual Message, now known as the State of the Union address, was delivered in the Senate chamber of New York City's Federal Hall. The US Constitution, which had come into force the previous year, allows the president to give Congress 'Information of the State of the Union and recommend to their consideration such measures as he shall judge necessary and expedient.'

This important speech gave the country's first president an opportunity to define his role as elected leader. Although he did not make any direct demands, he suggested establishing a permanent army, a national currency, standard weights and measures, and an educational system.

ALSO ON THIS DAY

1978

After three unsuccessful political campaigns, Harvey Milk is elected as a member of the San Francisco Board of Supervisors in 1978, becoming the first openly gay person elected to public office in California.

JANUARY

9

1983

BRITISH PM MARGARET THATCHER VISITS THE FALKLAND ISLANDS

Almost six months after Britain's victory in the Falklands War, in which Argentina had attempted to seize control of the South Atlantic colony, Prime Minister Margaret Thatcher stepped off the Royal Air Force Hercules cargo plane that had flown her 8,000 miles (13,000 km) to the archipelago. Her visit was top secret (the press only found out about it two hours after she set off) and had been six months in the

▲ Margaret Thatcher and her husband Denis (left) visit Stanley Junior School, Stanley, in the Falkland Islands, 1983.

planning. She spent five days on the islands, meeting the British troops stationed there and the islanders, who granted her the Freedom of the Falklands. Her premiership had been on the wane before the 74-day war, but it proved to be a turning point in her career, cementing her global celebrity and helping her attain re-election in 1983.

It was a crucial turning point in Thatcher's career.

JANUARY

10

630

PROPHET MUHAMMAD LEADS HIS ARMY TOWARDS MECCA

After years of fighting, the Meccan tribe of Quraysh signed the ten-year Treaty of Hudaybiyyah with the Muslim community of Medina: a pact not to instigate violence between opposing allies. There was a two-year period of peace before the Quraysh-allied tribe Banu Bakr attacked the Muslim-allied Banu Khuza. After learning of this treaty violation, Muslim leader Muhammad assembled the largest Muslim army ever seen, estimated at 10,000 strong, and marched towards the Quraysh's stronghold (and his own birthplace), Mecca. Using the element of surprise, he stormed the city from four sides. It was a relatively bloodless attack with only a few casualties. After the Muslims had taken the city and destroyed its idols, Muhammad declared it a place of sanctuary and the holiest site of Islam.

Scholars disagree on the precise date of this momentous event, some suggesting 11th December, 629 as another possibility. This uncertainty is due to the differing calendars in use in Mecca at the time.

11

1755

AMERICAN FOUNDING FATHER ALEXANDER HAMILTON IS BORN

He would go on to become one of the central figures of America's struggle for independence, as well as a revolutionary commander, a distinguished lawyer, the first Secretary of the Treasury and the creator of the US banking system; but Alexander Hamilton started life on the West Indian island of Nevis as the illegitimate child of Scottish businessman James Hamilton and Rachel Faucette. His father abandoned the family when Alexander was ten and his mother died of fever three years later. Hamilton became a ward of her family and had to earn his own keep in the accounts department of an import–export firm.

> **Hamilton would go on to become one of the central figures of America's struggle for independence.**

His intelligence and ambition saw him earn the favour of wealthy patrons, who sent him to America for a college education. It was in New York, while studying at what is now Columbia University, that Hamilton fell in with the radical revolutionary politics of the day.

JANUARY

12

1895

THE NATIONAL TRUST IS FOUNDED

When British social reformer Octavia Hill was asked to help preserve Sayes Court Garden in Southeast London from development, it set in motion the idea for the National Trust, a charity concerned with the preservation of land, buildings and other items of beauty or of historic, artistic and national interest. Hill, Sir Robert Hunter and Hardwicke Rawnsley worked together to found the Trust and just a few weeks after it was registered it was given its first piece of land: 5 acres (2 hectares) of clifftop in Wales, known as Dinas Oleu (Citadel of Light). Its first building, a 14th-century Wealden hall-house (a type of farmhouse traditional in southeast England), was acquired a year later. The Trust is now the largest membership organisation in the UK and one of the largest landowners, with more than 610,000 acres (248,000 hectares) of land and more than 500 historic houses and other properties in its portfolio.

The National Trust was an extension of Hill's work providing low-cost housing and social support to London's poor. It was through her time spent on these housing estates that she recognised the need for cultural stimulation and green spaces in urban areas.

JANUARY

13

86 BCE

ROMAN GENERAL AND CONSUL GAIUS MARIUS DIES

Often referred to as the 'third founder of Rome', Gaius Marius was one of the Republic's most accomplished figures, as a successful politician, military reformer and skilful general. He was beloved by the people for ending the long-running Jugurthine War in North Africa and leading an attack that crushed the mighty Cimbri tribe, preventing the fall of Rome. He was re-elected for the consulship an unprecedented seven times, but in old age he faced competition for military dominance from his subordinate, Sulla. The power struggle caused Sulla to exile Marius, but the ageing general wasn't done yet. He returned to Rome when Sulla was on a military expedition in the East and seized power once again, executing anyone who had supported his exile and tarnishing his reputation for good.

Gaius Marius was one of the Republic's most accomplished figures.

14

83 BCE

ROMAN POLITICIAN AND GENERAL MARK ANTONY IS BORN

Around the time that Gaius Marius was hanging up his sword, another iconic Roman general was finding his feet. In the years that followed, Mark Antony would become an accomplished soldier and one of Roman dictator Julius Caesar's closer confidants, defending his legacy and delivering the eulogy after Caesar's assassination on the Ides of March, and defeating two of Caesar's assassins, Brutus and Cassius, in battle. He did not share the same affection for Caesar's adopted son and heir, Octavian, later Augustus Caesar, whom he engaged on the battlefield. When Octavian's forces advanced on Alexandria in 30 BCE, Mark Antony fell on his sword after making a suicide pact with his lover, Egyptian Queen Cleopatra. Octavian would go on to rule Rome for the next 40 years.

▼ Mark Antony as depicted by the French artist Charles Joseph Natoire.

JANUARY
15
1534

KING HENRY VIII BECOMES HEAD OF THE CHURCH OF ENGLAND

Four years earlier, the Pope had refused to grant Henry VIII an annulment of his first marriage to Catherine of Aragon. Desperate to remarry and produce a son and heir, Henry took matters into his own hands. In his controversial Act of Supremacy, Henry declared himself head of the Church of England, marking the start of the English Reformation. The act also required that English subjects recognise the king's second marriage to Anne Boleyn. Catherine was soon banished from court and stripped of her titles. In the years that followed, Henry would disband the Catholic monasteries, priories, friaries and convents across his kingdom.

JANUARY
16
2006

ELLEN JOHNSON SIRLEAF BECOMES PRESIDENT OF LIBERIA

When Ellen Johnson Sirleaf stood in front of the Liberian flag in Monrovia and placed her left hand on the Bible, she made history as Africa's first elected female head of state. The Harvard-trained banker took over from an interim government that had been in place since 2003, when the warlord Charles Taylor fled after 14 years of brutal civil war. She faced the gargantuan task of rebuilding a country with limited infrastructure, no electrical grid and no piped water. Her inauguration was attended by thousands of Liberians, who cheered 'Queen of Africa', and a host of foreign dignitaries, including First Lady of the United States Laura Bush, US Secretary of State Condoleezza Rice and Nigerian President Olusegun Obasanjo.

ALSO ON THIS DAY

1559

Henry VIII's daughter, Elizabeth I, is crowned Queen of England in Westminster Abbey.

ALSO ON THIS DAY

1547

Ivan IV, 'The Terrible', Grand Duke of Muscovy, is crowned Tsar of Russia.

JANUARY

17

1961

PRESIDENT DWIGHT D. EISENHOWER ADDRESSES THE NATION

Dwight D. Eisenhower, the oldest president in a century, was handing over the reigns of American power to the youngest president ever elected: John F. Kennedy. Three days before leaving office, Eisenhower made a televised farewell speech in which he warned against the over-militarisation of a country facing a 'hostile ideology' in which the war machine would come to dictate foreign policy. In the midst of the Cold War and the ever-present fears of the American people about Russian nuclear rearmament and Sputnik, Eisenhower was the voice of reason. "In the councils of government, we must guard against the acquisition of unwarranted influence, whether sought or unsought, by the military-industrial complex," he said.

> " The potential for the disastrous rise of misplaced power exists and will persist. "

The president left behind him eight years of leadership in which he had helped to end the Korean War, expanded social security and established NASA.

JANUARY

18

1591

KING NARESUAN DEFEATS CROWN PRINCE MINCHIT
King Naresuan of Siam killed Crown Prince Minchit Sra of Burma in single combat at Nong Sarai, Thailand.

JANUARY

19

1966

INDIRA GANDHI IS ELECTED
Gandhi became India's first female head of government and the second democratically elected female prime minister in the world.

JANUARY

20

1869

FIRST WOMAN TESTIFIES BEFORE THE US CONGRESS
Women's rights campaigner Elizabeth Cady Stanton spoke about why women need to be enfranchised.

JANUARY

21

1952

NEHRU'S PARTY WINS THE GENERAL ELECTION
Jawaharlal Nehru's Congress party won India's first general election with 364 of the 489 seats.

JANUARY

22

1931

NEW GOVERNOR-GENERAL OF AUSTRALIA IS SWORN IN
Sir Isaac Isaacs, the country's first Australian-born Governor-General, is sworn in, despite controversy.

JANUARY

23

1368

ZHU YUANZHANG IS CROWNED EMPEROR When Yuanzhang was crowned Hongwi Emperor, he founded China's last Han-led imperial dynasty.

JANUARY

24

1968

SIR WINSTON CHURCHILL DIES Held six days after his death, the former British prime minister's state funeral was the largest in history at that time.

JANUARY
25
1941

DATE SET FOR MARCH ON WASHINGTON MOVEMENT

In 1925, American civil rights campaigner A. Philip Randolph helped to organise the Brotherhood of Sleeping Car Porters – a labour union for African-American Pullman Company employees. He led the union for ten years, arguing for wage increases and an end to discriminatory practices, before serving as president of the National Negro Congress. But he is remembered chiefly for the idea of a march on Washington, DC, organised and led by African-Americans to protest segregation in the armed forces. With an estimated 100,000 people expected at the 1st July, 1941 march, pressure mounted on President Franklin D. Roosevelt to legislate change. The march was cancelled after the president issued Executive Order 8802, prohibiting discrimination in federal vocational and training programmes and in government-contracted defence industries.

With an estimated 100,000 people expected at the march, pressure mounted on President Franklin D. Roosevelt to legislate change.

JANUARY
26
1950

DR RAJENDRA PRASAD BECOMES PRESIDENT OF INDIA

After 100 years of British rule, a public holiday was declared to mark the day when the independent Republic of India became a reality. It followed more than two years of turbulence after Britain transferred power back to the country in 1947. Prasad was a key campaigner, alongside Mahatma Gandhi, in the nationalist movement. In his speech to the crowds, taking over as head of state from King George VI, he spoke in Hindi and English, saying:

" Today, for the first time in our long and chequered history, we find the whole of this vast land ... brought together under the jurisdiction of one constitution and one union. "

Prasad served two terms as president, the only Indian president to do so.

22

GENERAL YUE FEI IS EXECUTED IN HANGZHOU

Yue Fei is a legendary figure from the war that broke out in 12th-century China between the invading Jurchen tribesmen of the Jin Empire and the Southern Song court. While the young Song emperor Song Gaozong was advised by courtier Qin Gui to consolidate the south and relinquish the northern territories to the Jurchen, one of his generals, Yue Fei, refused to surrender, and pushed his troops to keep fighting northwards, winning many victories. Eventually the Song signed a peace treaty with the Jin and Yue Fei was recalled from the front lines to the Song capital in present-day Hangzhou. There he was accused of insubordination and stripped of his rank. Shortly after, he was found dead in his cell, having been poisoned or strangled (accounts differ), supposedly under the orders of Qin Gui.

▶ A wall painting in the Yue Fei Temple, China, portrays Yue Fei.

JANUARY

28

814

DEATH OF THE FIRST HOLY ROMAN EMPEROR

Charles the Great, or Charlemagne, heralded as King of the Franks and 'father of Europe', was the first person to hold the title of Holy Roman Emperor; it was given to him by Pope Leo III, who was grateful that the ruler had restored him to power. The emperor's military conquests meant that by the time of his death he dominated Europe, converting the masses to Christianity as he went. He was also an advocate of the arts and education, making reforms across his empire. He helped boost trade and commerce by introducing a common silver currency and standardising weights and measures. He was in the now-German spa town of Aachen when he died, possibly of pleurisy. He was succeeded by his son, Louis the Pious.

ALSO ON THIS DAY

1547

King Henry VIII of England dies and is succeeded by his nine-year-old son, Edward VI.

JANUARY

29

1891

QUEEN LILIUOKALANI IS PROCLAIMED THE LAST MONARCH OF HAWAII

Born in 1838, Queen Liliuokalani came from a well-to-do Hawaiian family; her mother was an advisor to King Kamehameha III. Her brother was elected king before her (it was from him that she inherited the throne in 1891) and had signed away much of the monarchy's power in the 'Bayonet Constitution' under pressure from American settlers. Only two years after Liliuokalani's reign began, after she refused to recognise the new constitution, an American military-backed coup led by Sanford Dole, whose brother James would start the Hawaiian Pineapple Company in 1901, took over the Hawaiian government. To avoid any bloodshed, Liliuokalani surrendered and spent the rest of her life in exile advocating for a free Hawaii.

> Liliuokalani surrendered and spent the rest of her life in exile advocating for a free Hawaii.

JANUARY

30

1703

47 RŌNIN AVENGE THE DEATH OF THEIR MASTER

The rōnin cut off Kira's head and laid it on Asano's grave to restore their master's honour.

When daimyō lord Asano Naganori of Akō was offended by senior court official Kira Yoshinaka in the shōgun's residence, he cut him in the face – a capital offence in feudal Japan. His punishment was *seppuku* – ritual suicide – and his family was left with nothing. This left 47 of his most loyal samurai knights, under the command of Ôishi Kuranosuke, feeling vengeful, and they hatched a plan to punish Kira. To avoid suspicion, they split up, taking new jobs and continuing with their daily lives. Some of the men even worked in Kira's home. Then, one morning, they stormed the residence, and when Kira refused to commit seppuku, Ôishi cut off his head and laid it on Asano's grave to restore his master's honour. The 47 rōnin (masterless samurai) turned themselves in, were convicted of murder and received seppuku as their punishment.

JANUARY

31

1606

GUY FAWKES JUMPS TO HIS DEATH

Guy Fawkes was a key conspirator in the English Catholic plot to bring down Protestant King James I and his government in 1605. Fawkes had joined the group, led by Robert Catesby, in 1594 after spending a few years fighting in the Eighty Years' War as a member of the Catholic Spanish army. Fawkes was responsible for lighting the fuse that would ignite 36 barrels filled with gunpowder hidden in the cellars below the Houses of Parliament – but the plan was foiled when Fawkes was caught red-handed guarding the gunpowder. After being tortured for two days he signed a confession and was sentenced to be hung, drawn and quartered. But on the day the hanging was to take place, he jumped from the scaffold, breaking his own neck.

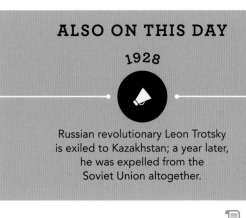

ALSO ON THIS DAY

1928

Russian revolutionary Leon Trotsky is exiled to Kazakhstan; a year later, he was expelled from the Soviet Union altogether.

CHAPTER

2

February

FEBRUARY
1
1587

QUEEN ELIZABETH I SIGNS THE DEATH WARRANT FOR HER COUSIN, MARY, QUEEN OF SCOTS

Protestant Elizabeth I had already seen off one Catholic – her sister, Mary I of England – to claim her place on the English throne in 1558 (for her coronation, see above, 15th January). But there were many Catholics in England and across Europe who believed she was illegitimate. They saw Scotland's queen, Mary Stuart, as the rightful ruler. This Mary was Henry VIII's great-niece; her grandmother was Margaret Tudor, Henry's sister. The teenage Mary was married to the short-lived King Francis II of France, making her a powerful threat to the English queen's throne. After her husband's death in 1560, Mary returned to Scotland to claim her throne and demanded Elizabeth name her as her heir. Elizabeth refused and years of animosity followed.

Mary strengthened her claim to the throne by marrying another of Margaret Tudor's grandchildren, Henry Stuart, Lord Darnley, and then giving birth to a son and heir in 1566. But things soon went downhill for the Scottish queen when her husband was murdered and she was implicated in the crime. She was forced to abdicate the throne and was placed in custody in England.

Though Elizabeth was shocked at the queen's treatment, she soon realised the benefits of Mary's imprisonment. When plots to replace Elizabeth with Mary on the English throne came to light, it was Mary who took the brunt of the country's wrath. She stood accused of treason but refused to admit any wrongdoing and ask the queen's forgiveness, leaving Elizabeth with little choice but to find her guilty. A week after she signed the death warrant, Mary's head was cut off in three blows.

▶ Elizabeth I of England decrees the death of Mary Stuart, Queen of Scots.

FEBRUARY

2

1970

ANTI-WAR ACTIVIST BERTRAND RUSSELL DIES OF INFLUENZA

Though he was a celebrated philosopher and Nobel Prize-winning writer, Russell is perhaps best known for his passionate political activism. He was a leading light in opposing World War I and the Vietnam War. In 1918 he was sent to prison for six months for writing an article for the pacifist journal *The Tribunal*. Much later in life, he was one of the earliest high-profile supporters of the Campaign for Nuclear Disarmament. In 1961, after leading a mass anti-nuclear sit-in in Trafalgar Square in London, he received a second prison sentence; he was 89 years old. Throughout his life Russell was involved in supporting suffragists, promoting freedom of religion and railing against nationalism and political persecution.

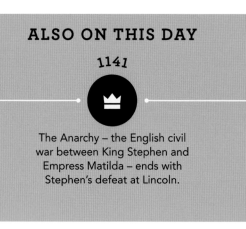

ALSO ON THIS DAY

1141

The Anarchy – the English civil war between King Stephen and Empress Matilda – ends with Stephen's defeat at Lincoln.

FEBRUARY

3

1960

BRITISH PM ADDRESSES THE PARLIAMENT OF SOUTH AFRICA

When Harold Macmillan made his speech to the MPs in Cape Town's Houses of Parliament, it was the first clear acknowledgment from the British government that the imperial era was over and African independence was on the horizon. In the month before the shocking Sharpeville Massacre, it also made clear that apartheid, though it would continue for another 30 years, was strongly opposed by the international community. In Cape Town, after a month of touring the African continent, Macmillan received a frosty reception, with many politicians refusing to applaud his speech, in which he famously said:

> " **The wind of change is blowing through this continent, and whether we like it or not, this growth of national consciousness is a political fact. We must all accept it as a fact, and our national policies must take account of it.** "

FEBRUARY
4
1866

MARY BAKER EDDY CURES HERSELF THROUGH PRAYER

The day before, Mary Baker Eddy (then Mary Patterson) had slipped on some ice in Lynn, Massachusetts. She was reportedly suffering from internal injuries that brought on spasms and incredible pain. Pain was nothing new to Eddy, who suffered from dyspepsia. The devout Christian had taken a keen interest in science and healing, trying a number of alternative therapies such as unusual diets, hydropathy and homeopathy, while taking comfort in the Bible. The day after her fall, believing she might die, Eddy turned to Matthew 9:2 – in which Jesus cures a man 'sick of the palsy' – and claimed she was healed almost immediately. She described it as:

> [T]he falling apple that led me to the discovery [of] how to be well myself, and how to make others so.

Nine years later she would publish *Science and Health with Key to the Scriptures*, a companion to the Bible for Christian Scientists.

FEBRUARY
5
1788

BRITISH PM AND SOCIAL REFORMER ROBERT PEEL IS BORN

Widely acknowledged as the founder of the British Conservative Party, Robert Peel was the son of a wealthy cotton mill owner and had received the finest education money could buy. He joined Parliament in 1809, his father effectively buying him his seat in the House of Commons. Despite his silver-spoon background, Peel worked hard and became Home Secretary in 1822. It was during this tenure that he made significant reforms to the penal code, reducing the number of crimes punishable by death, providing payment for jailers and offering education for inmates. In 1829 he created London's Metropolitan Police – earning police officers the nickname 'Bobby'. He came to power as prime minister for the first time in 1834 and was elected again in 1841. He passed the Mines Act and the Factory Act, which banned employers from hiring women and children to work underground and limited the hours they could work in factories.

FEBRUARY

6

2017

65TH ANNIVERSARY OF QUEEN ELIZABETH II BECOMING MONARCH

Princess Elizabeth was staying at the royal hunting lodge in Kenya when her father, King George VI, died in his sleep in 1952 after a fatal coronary thrombosis – the 56-year-old was also suffering from lung cancer. The queen, who was just 25, returned home immediately to take on the role of head of state. She became Britain's longest-reigning monarch in September 2015, after spending 63 years and 216 days on the throne, surpassing her great-great-grandmother Queen Victoria's record. Her Sapphire Jubilee was marked with an official photograph in which she wore sapphire jewellery given to her by her father on her wedding in 1947.

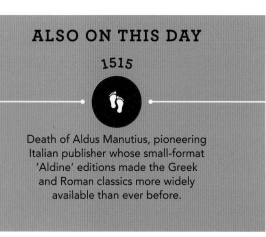

ALSO ON THIS DAY

1515

Death of Aldus Manutius, pioneering Italian publisher whose small-format 'Aldine' editions made the Greek and Roman classics more widely available than ever before.

FEBRUARY

7

1819

RAFFLES LEAVES SINGAPORE AFTER SIGNING TREATY

On 6th February the recently knighted Sir Thomas Stamford Raffles, who had previously been instrumental in seizing control of Dutch-occupied Java and ruling there as lieutenant governor, signed a treaty with the *temenggong* (governor) of Singapore, Abdu'r Rahman, and Hussein Shah, Sultan of Johor, giving the British East India Company the right to set up a trading post on the island of Singapore. The temenggong and sultan would receive annual payments in exchange.

The treaty allowed a trading post to be set up on the island in exchange for annual payments.

The British flag was formally hoisted while many of the island's 1,000 inhabitants watched as the treaty, written in English and Malay, was signed. The next day, Raffles set sail for Bengkulu in Indonesia. He would not return for three years, and he died in 1826, but his place in Singaporean history was already cemented.

FEBRUARY

8

1903

'FATHER OF MALAYSIA', TUNKU ABDUL RAHMAN, IS BORN

Abdul Rahman was an unlikely first prime minister of Malaysia. He was born into a country under British control; he was the 20th child of the Malayan sultan and his fourth wife; and his young adulthood was a catalogue of educational failures. But, while studying in the UK, he set up the Malay Society of Great Britain – his first foray into international diplomacy. He later became leader of the Alliance Party and the first chief minister of Malaya.

In January 1956 he travelled to London where he successfully negotiated Malayan independence and went on to hold the post of prime minister, both of Malaya and then, from 1963, of the Federation of Malaysia.

▼ Tunku Abdul Rahman reads the Proclamation of Independence in 1957.

FEBRUARY

9

1907

MILLICENT FAWCETT TAKES TO THE STREETS FOR THE MUD MARCH

'Great demonstration', the flyer read, 'before the opening of Parliament to demand the Franchise.' The women planned to meet at Hyde Park Corner and march to Exeter Hall for a rally including a speech by Millicent Fawcett, president of the non-militant National Union of Women's Suffrage Societies, and featuring an all-female orchestra. It was the first large march organised by the Union, but the weather didn't get that memo, and the rain came down with as much enthusiasm as the marchers (the event duly became known as the Mud March). Three thousand showed up in support, representing 40 suffrage organisations from across the social spectrum, and the march's success established the large-scale peaceful protest as a key tactic for the suffrage movement.

❝ **Courage calls to courage everywhere, and its voice cannot be denied.** ❞

MILLICENT FAWCETT

FEBRUARY

10

1840

QUEEN VICTORIA MARRIES PRINCE ALBERT

London's St James's Palace was the venue, nearby Buckingham Palace hosted the reception, and the cake weighed 136 kilograms (300 lbs). Queen Victoria had fallen for her German cousin, whom she had first met at her 17th birthday party, and had asked him to marry her – as was the protocol – in 1839.

At 1 pm Albert was escorted into the Chapel Royal by a Life Guards squadron.

❝ **I felt so happy when the ring was put on, and by my precious Albert.** ❞

QUEEN VICTORIA

The queen arrived by carriage moments later, dressed in a white silk satin dress trimmed with Honiton lace. She was carrying orange blossoms, a fertility symbol, and wore a sapphire brooch given to her by her husband-to-be. The blossoms did their job – the couple went on to have nine children. Theirs was considered one of the great royal marriages, full of love and passion. When Albert died unexpectedly in 1861, aged just 42, Victoria was devastated. She dressed in mourning for the remaining 40 years of her life.

FEBRUARY

11

1990

ANTI-APARTHEID CAMPAIGNER NELSON MANDELA IS FREED AFTER 27 YEARS IN PRISON

In 1964, Nelson Mandela, the deputy president of the African National Congress (ANC) in South Africa, was sentenced to life imprisonment along with seven other leaders for sabotage and conspiring to violently overthrow the state. He spent 18 years of his sentence on Robben Island, performing hard labour in a lime quarry, before eventually being moved to Victor Verster prison in the Western Cape province. Mandela had refused previous offers of early release, unwilling to submit to conditions that would restrict his and his party's actions.

After serving more than a quarter of a century behind bars, he was finally able to walk free unconditionally. Mandela was greeted by huge crowds. That evening the 71-year-old addressed 50,000 people who had gathered outside Cape Town's City Hall. He stood on the balcony and declared:

> **Our struggle has reached a decisive moment. Our march to freedom is irreversible.**

Four years later, in the first national elections after apartheid ended in 1994, he was voted in as the country's new president.

◀ Nelson Mandela speaks in the rotunda of the US Capitol in Washington, DC, on 23rd September, 1998.

FEBRUARY

12

1909

FOUNDATION OF THE NAACP

The NAACP aimed to secure an end to slavery, equal protection under the law and suffrage for all men.

The National Association for the Advancement of Colored People (NAACP) was founded in the wake of the 1908 anti-black race riot in Springfield, Illinois. A group of white liberals, including Mary White Ovington, William English Walling, Dr Henry Moscowitz and Oswald Garrison Villard, put out a call to encourage people to come forward to discuss racial justice. Seven of the 60 original members were African-American, including W. E. B. Du Bois, Ida B. Wells, Archibald Grimké and Mary Church Terrell. The group came together for the first time on what would have been President Abraham Lincoln's 100th birthday. The organisation aimed to secure an end to slavery, equal protection under the law and suffrage for all men. The group established its headquarters in New York City in 1910. Du Bois, who served as director of publications and research, was the only African-American among the organisation's original executive team.

FEBRUARY

13

1861

ABRAHAM LINCOLN IS DECLARED US PRESIDENT

Lincoln almost didn't make it to his own inauguration. With civil war on the horizon, the soon-to-be president of the United States was the target of an assassination plot, which was poised to snuff him out as he travelled through Baltimore by train on his way to Washington, DC. Ten days after the electoral college confirmed he had rightfully won the election of 6th November, 1860, he arrived in Washington under a veil of secrecy. The Pinkerton private detective agency had foiled the would-be assassins, by dressing Lincoln in a disguise and rearranging his travel plans so he arrived in Baltimore in the middle of the night. He would not be so lucky four years later when John Wilkes Booth shot Lincoln in the head at Ford's Theater, Washington.

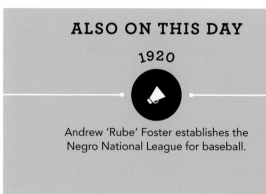

ALSO ON THIS DAY

1920

Andrew 'Rube' Foster establishes the Negro National League for baseball.

FEBRUARY

14
1831

FORMER MEXICAN PRESIDENT IS EXECUTED

Vicente Guerrero rose to power through the ranks of the Mexican revolutionary forces. Independence leader José Maria Morelos had tasked him with promoting the independence movement in southwestern Mexico and Guerrero did not disappoint – even after Morelos' execution, he continued to fight against the Spanish until independence was achieved in 1821. In 1829 he was elected as the second president of an independent Mexico. His People's Party had campaigned on the introduction of public schools, land title reforms and other liberal policies that helped the poor. Guerrero, who was himself part African Mexican and part Amerindian, championed the rights of Mexico's racially oppressed, formally abolishing slavery in that year. But his policies were unpopular with conservatives, and after eight months in power he was overthrown. After a year of evading capture, Guerrero was eventually arrested, court-martialed and convicted of treason. His punishment was execution by firing squad.

FEBRUARY

15
399 BCE

SOCRATES IS SENTENCED
After the City of Athens found Socrates guilty of 'impiety' and 'corrupting the young', he was sentenced to death and forced to drink poison.

FEBRUARY

16
1959

CASTRO IS SWORN IN AS PM OF CUBA Castro became prime minster after he led the resistance against Fulgencio Batista's seven-year military rule.

FEBRUARY

17
1969

GOLDA MEIR IS SWORN IN AS PM OF ISRAEL Meir was Israel's first female prime minister and was the first person to receive an Israeli passport in 1974.

FEBRUARY

18
259 BCE

QIN SHI HUANG IS BORN
Qin Shi was the first emperor of the Qin dynasty and one of the most important leaders in Chinese history – he ruled from 246 to 210 BCE.

FEBRUARY

19
1915

GOPAL KRISHNA GOKHALE DIES Indian National Congress president Gokhale founded the Servants of India Society in 1905 to help the underprivileged.

FEBRUARY

20
1895

FREDERICK DOUGLASS DIES
Douglass remained an activist right up until he died – earlier that day he had been attending a meeting of the National Council of Women.

FEBRUARY

21
1965

MALCOLM X IS ASSASSINATED
The African-American nationalist and religious leader was shot in the Audubon ballroom in New York by members of the Nation of Islam.

FEBRUARY
22
1844

LOUIS BRAILLE'S ALPHABET IS FIRST DEMONSTRATED

At the dedication ceremony for a new building for the Royal Institution for Blind Youths in Paris, Assistant Director Joseph Guadet demonstrated Louis Braille's code. The date is considered to mark the birth of braille, which the blind student had started developing some 20 years before. He had been inspired to do so after army captain Charles Barbier had visited the school to demonstrate a tactile system for soldiers to communicate without speaking. Braille had figured out 63 ways to use a six-dot cell in an area the size of a fingertip. He went on to become a teacher at the Institution. In 1852 he died of tuberculosis, and two years later his code was adopted as the official communications system for blind people in France.

FEBRUARY
23
1836

THE SIEGE OF THE ALAMO BEGINS

Mexican general Antonio López de Santa Anna declared himself the 'Napoleon of the West', routinely changing his political stance and seizing power during Mexico's unstable years as a newly independent country. He served as president 11 times between 1833 and 1855 and was also a military-backed dictator. The Battle of the Alamo – the now-famous mission and fortress compound in San Antonio, Texas – which lasted for 13 days, was a key turning point in the Texas Revolution. Texas, then under Mexican control, was opposed to Santa Anna's regime and was seeking to become a republic. The dictator's slaughter of Texan forces, after the siege ended, inspired many people to take up arms in the fight for independence.

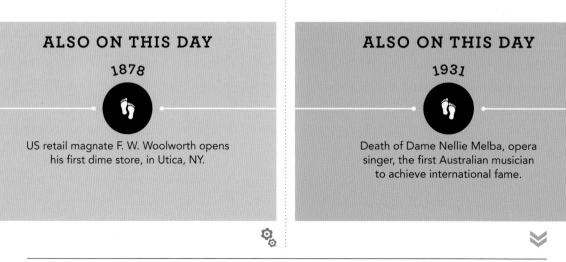

ALSO ON THIS DAY

1878

US retail magnate F. W. Woolworth opens his first dime store, in Utica, NY.

ALSO ON THIS DAY

1931

Death of Dame Nellie Melba, opera singer, the first Australian musician to achieve international fame.

▼ The Texan defenders of the Alamo fighting Mexican soldiers. Davy Crockett died in the siege. He is pictured here, centre right, with his rifle above his head.

GENERAL JUAN PERÓN IS ELECTED PRESIDENT OF ARGENTINA FOR THE FIRST TIME

In October 1945, Juan Perón, freshly released from custody, addressed a crowd 300,000 strong from the presidential palace and vowed to represent the people of Argentina in the upcoming presidential elections. It wasn't his first foray into power – he had previously been secretary of labour and vice president, before being ousted in a coup. Four days after he made his announcement, he married his greatest political ally – Eva Duarte, later known as Evita – whose support and influence would lead him to victory in February the following year. With his new bride by his side, Perón's popularity soared as he sought a self-sufficient vision for Argentina. He would remain in power until after his wife's sudden death in 1952, before a military coup put an end to his first presidency. It would be more than 20 years until Perón returned to power.

▼ President Juan Perón and his wife Eva Perón celebrate the Día de la Lealtad, or Loyalty Day, in Argentina, 17th October, 1951.

PETER BENENSON, FOUNDER OF AMNESTY INTERNATIONAL, DIES

In 1961, British lawyer Peter Benenson had started a one-year 'Appeal for Amnesty' – a campaign to release six 'forgotten prisoners' of conscience. He had been outraged after hearing about two students in Portugal who had been sentenced to seven years in prison for drinking a toast to liberty. It started a worldwide human rights movement. Sixteen years after its founding, the organisation was awarded the Nobel Peace Prize. Benenson, who worked on a number of human rights issues and campaigns during his lifetime, also established the British branch of the International Commission of Jurists, Justice. He was 83 at the time of his death, by which time his legacy, Amnesty International, had 1.8 million members.

Benson had been outraged after hearing about two students in Portugal who had been sentenced to seven years in prison for drinking a toast to liberty.

U THANT SIGNS EARTH DAY PROCLAMATION

UN secretary general, U Thant's proclamation established 21st March as Earth Day to coincide with the vernal equinox; the first one had been held the previous year. In his statement, he said:

> **May there only be peaceful and cheerful Earth Days to come for our beautiful Spaceship Earth as it continues to spin and circle in frigid space with its warm and fragile cargo of animate life.**

Since that first Earth Day, the UN marks the occasion by ringing the Peace Bell every year at its headquarters in New York at the exact moment of the vernal equinox. Earth Day was the idea of community activist and newspaper publisher John McConnell to remind us of our shared responsibility for the environment. The date, which is the northern hemisphere's first day of spring and the southern hemisphere's first day of fall, was chosen because it is a day of renewal.

FEBRUARY
27
1900

THE UK'S LABOUR PARTY IS FORMED

Keir Hardie came from humble beginnings: he had worked from the age of eight and was a coal miner by 11. Having taught himself to read and write, the Scotsman established a union at the colliery where he worked, leading the first-ever Lanarkshire miners' strike in 1881. He stood for the Independent Labour Party, a precursor to the Labour Party, in the 1892 general election and won a seat in Parliament. Hardie's radical point of view was heavily criticised: he supported women's rights, Indian self-rule and old-age pensions, and routinely criticised the monarchy. The various left-wing organisations came together in 1900 to form a single party to sponsor parliamentary candidates, with Hardie at the helm. He was one of just two Labour Party MPs who won seats in 1900. When he resigned his leadership a decade later, there were 40.

> **Hardie's radical point of view was heavily criticised: he supported women's rights, Indian self-rule and old-age pensions.**

FEBRUARY
28
1784

JOHN WESLEY ORDAINS THE FIRST METHODIST PRIESTS

John Wesley was a Church of England minister who went against the grain by preaching outdoors to crowds of working-class people. This approach was looked down upon by many people and Wesley faced a backlash, both from other ministers and from the press. The term 'Methodist' comes from Wesley's university days when he met with other Christians for Bible study and prayer; their methodical approach to their faith earned the 'Holy Club' members their nickname. Wesley had initially wanted to remain within the fold of the Anglican Church, but when the Church of England refused to have a bishop ordain Dr Thomas Coke, whom Wesley was sending to America to preach, he started to break away, ordaining Coke himself and establishing a structure for Methodists to ensure that the movement would continue after him. It is estimated that there are 70 million Methodists around the world today.

29
1988

ARCHBISHOP DESMOND TUTU IS ARRESTED

Archbishop Desmond Tutu was a prominent figure in the fight against apartheid in South Africa. Tutu was leading a protest march in Cape Town against the government's ban on anti-apartheid activities when he, along with his wife and 80 others, was arrested. The previous week, the government had announced new measures that sought to stifle the voices and actions of the United Democratic Front and the Congress of South African Trade Unions. Tutu spent two hours in custody before being released without charge. The archbishop had been awarded the Nobel Peace Prize four years before for his work in the region. Tutu told the press after he was released:

" **What we did today was not the negative thing of saying we disobey, it was the positive thing of saying we are obeying God.** "

◀ Archbishop Desmond Tutu carries a cross in Johannesburg, South Africa, on 31st May, 1988.

CHAPTER

3

March

MARCH
1
1872

PRESIDENT ULYSSES S. GRANT ESTABLISHES THE WORLD'S FIRST NATIONAL PARK

In late 1871 a park bill was promoted in Washington, DC. Inspired by the 1864 Yosemite Act, which had protected Yosemite Valley in California from settlement, this new bill sought to do the same, indefinitely, in the Yellowstone region. Explorers and artists, with their tales, photographs and sketches, helped to persuade Congress that this was an area of outstanding natural beauty that needed legal protection. While Grant's prowess as a military leader is undisputed, the environmental legacy he left by signing into law Yellowstone National Park – the first of what would become 418 areas covering some 85 million acres (34 million hectares) – is of signal importance, paving the way for the protection of nature for centuries to come.

▼ Entrance to Yellowstone Park, circa 1900.

MARCH
2
1855

ALEXANDER II BECOMES EMPEROR OF RUSSIA

After the death of his conservative father, Nicholas I, Alexander Nikolaevich Romanov (Tsar Alexander II) was a breath of fresh air for the Russian people. The Crimean War was still in progress, and Alexander recognised change was necessary if the country was to recover from the conflict. In 1861 he abolished serfdom – the arrangement by which Russian peasants were tied to the estates on which they toiled for rich landlords. Under Alexander, the serfs now had freedom of movement – in theory, even though financially they had little choice.

> " Better to abolish serfdom from above than wait [for the time when] it begins to abolish itself from below. "
>
> ALEXANDER II

His other key reforms included loosening censorship laws, modernising the armed forces and improving the country's education system. He favoured peace over war, joining with Germany and Austria in the League of the Three Emperors to stabilise relations in Europe, while still managing to expand Russia's empire.

MARCH
3
1887

ANNE SULLIVAN BEGINS TEACHING HELEN KELLER

When Helen Keller died in 1968, she had left an indelible mark on the world, helping to change public perception of people with disabilities. But the public speaker and author's journey on that path began when she was introduced to her teacher, Anne Sullivan. Sullivan had first-hand experience of disability, having suffered from impaired vision after an infection as a child. Her weakened eyesight had improved in the years since, but when, aged 21, she met six-year-old Keller, she was able to empathise with the child, who could neither see, hear nor speak. Sullivan imparted to Keller her pioneering touch-teaching techniques and the child went on to learn how to read, write and speak. Thanks to Sullivan, Keller attended Radcliffe College in Cambridge, Massachusetts, graduating in 1904. The two remained constant companions until Sullivan's death in 1936.

Keller helped to change the public perception of people with disabilities.

MARCH
4
1193

MUSLIM SULTAN SALADIN DIES

During the Crusades, Saladin's leadership of the Muslim military resulted in a number of decisive victories over the European Crusaders, most notably at the triumphant Battle of Hattin in 1187. It was as a result of that battle that the Muslims were able to retake Jerusalem and other significant Holy Land cities. But the medieval series of wars was relentless, and when King Richard I of England was leading a coalition of Christian forces in the Third Crusade, it proved too much for the ageing sultan and his feudal conscripts, who would only commit to fighting for part of the year. After Saladin successfully negotiated the Treaty of Jaffa, retaining control over Jerusalem, King Richard headed back to England in October 1192, and Saladin rode home to Damascus where he died a few months later.

MARCH
5
1616

COPERNICUS' TREATISE IS BANNED BY THE CATHOLIC CHURCH

Nicolaus Copernicus was a Polish mathematician and astronomer who had come up with a revolutionary model of the universe that suggested the Sun was at the centre of the universe, rather than the Earth. The book in which he published his findings, *De revolutionibus orbium coelestium* (On the Revolutions of Celestial Bodies), came out just before his death in 1543. Although it may not have been widely read, it was later put on the Catholic Church's Index of Forbidden Books, where it remained until 1758. Though he was not the first to suggest such a model, Copernicus lends his name to the Copernican Revolution that ensued – a general scientific shift in thinking towards his 'heliocentric' (Sun-centred) model.

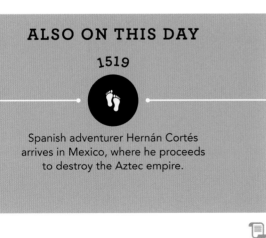

ALSO ON THIS DAY

1519

Spanish adventurer Hernán Cortés arrives in Mexico, where he proceeds to destroy the Aztec empire.

ALSO ON THIS DAY

1953

Soviet dictator Joseph Stalin dies from a cerebral haemorrhage.

MARCH

6

1933

FIRST LADY ELEANOR ROOSEVELT HOLDS
THE FIRST WHITE HOUSE PRESS CONFERENCE

Two days after her husband became president, Eleanor Roosevelt became the first person to hold a press conference at the White House. After her friend Lorena Hickok, a journalist for the Associated Press, made the suggestion, Roosevelt invited 35 women journalists into the Red Room for what would become the first of 348 press conferences she would attend during her husband's presidency. 'There weren't enough chairs to go around, so some had to sit on the floor,' she said of that first meeting. The press conferences, though not overtly political, provided valuable stories for the female reporters and gave Eleanor a national platform.

When her husband died suddenly from a cerebral haemorrhage in 1945, Roosevelt was the most active first lady the country had known. She had frequently travelled with him, even visiting troops during World War II. She had also given the American people a rare insight into the life of a first lady through her regular column, which was published between 1935 and 1962 and titled 'My Day'. At its peak it appeared in 90 papers across the country.

▼ Members of the first press conference held by Eleanor Roosevelt in 1933 pose with her at a luncheon by the Women's National Press Club on 14th March, 1946.

MARCH

7

1965

JOHN LEWIS LEADS A MARCH FROM SELMA TO MONTGOMERY

John Lewis was 25 years old when he led over 600 marchers across the Edmund Pettus Bridge in Selma, Alabama, on the way to Montgomery. The march was organised to demonstrate African-American citizens' desire to exercise their voting rights, which were largely hampered by racial discrimination. Lewis had been president of the Student Nonviolent Coordinating Committee two years earlier and one of the 'Big Six' – the leaders who organised the March on Washington, DC, where Dr Martin Luther King Jr delivered his 'I have a dream' speech. Together with the Reverend Hosea Williams and the other demonstrators, he tried to cross the bridge. The group was confronted by the Alabama State Troopers who released teargas and violently assaulted the crowd, injuring nearly 70 people and galvanising the public to travel to Selma for another march two days later.

The group was confronted by the Alabama State Troopers who released teargas and violently assaulted the crowd.

MARCH

8

1884

SUSAN B. ANTHONY ADDRESSES THE HOUSE JUDICIARY COMMITTEE

On what is now International Women's Day, 16 years after legislators introduced a federal women's suffrage amendment, Susan B. Anthony addressed the committee to argue for granting women the right to vote. "We appear before you this morning…," she said,

> **[T]o ask that you will, at your earliest convenience, report to the House in favour of the submission of a Sixteenth Amendment to the Legislatures of the several States, that shall prohibit the disfranchisement of citizens of the United States on account of sex.**

Anthony, together with Elizabeth Cady Stanton, was a co-founder of the National Woman Suffrage Association. Although the 19th Amendment was passed 14 years after her death, it was still nicknamed the Anthony Amendment.

MARCH

9

1954

BROADCASTER EDWARD R. MURROW CRITICISES JOSEPH MCCARTHY

The half-hour episode of *See It Now* was titled 'A Report on Senator Joseph McCarthy' and contained excerpts from McCarthy's own speeches. It sought to shine a light on the senator and show how he often contradicted himself. But it was a risky business. McCarthy was at the height of his power – for four years he had been terrorising the government, making wild and vast accusations of Soviet collusion, and branding powerful people as communist traitors, often on the basis of hearsay evidence. Edward R. Murrow's measured, carefully researched and brave journalistic attack on the senator was one of the harshest blows he was dealt and is considered the first step on the way to ending McCarthy's reign of terror.

MARCH

10

1783

THE REVOLUTIONARY WAR'S LAST NAVAL BATTLE IS FOUGHT

Hailed as the 'Father of the American Navy', Captain John Barry was the force's first commissioned officer, who started out as a cabin boy and wound up in charge of the fleet. Arguably the most successful command of his career was on board the 32-gun frigate *Alliance* during the Revolutionary War. In 1783, *Alliance* and *Duc de Lauzun* were charged with transporting 72,000 silver dollars from Cuba to the American colonies – wages for the war's soldiers, some of whom had not been paid in years. South of Cape Canaveral, a British squadron of three ships caught sight of them and engaged the *Alliance*. Barry's plan and accomplished naval tactics made it the last naval battle of the war.

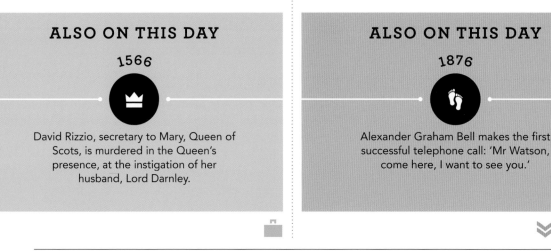

ALSO ON THIS DAY

1566

David Rizzio, secretary to Mary, Queen of Scots, is murdered in the Queen's presence, at the instigation of her husband, Lord Darnley.

ALSO ON THIS DAY

1876

Alexander Graham Bell makes the first successful telephone call: 'Mr Watson, come here, I want to see you.'

GORBACHEV BECOMES LEADER OF THE USSR'S COMMUNIST PARTY

" **The Soviet people want full-blooded and unconditional democracy.** "

MIKHAIL GORBACHEV

After just one year in power, Konstantin Chernenko died on 10th March of a smoking-related illness. He was the third Russian leader to die in as many years and the Soviet Union was in need of a new leader. Mikhail Gorbachev, who had been slowly rising through the ranks of the Communist Party, was more than happy to fill the void. The new general secretary came from humble beginnings, the son of peasant farmers, but he was intelligent and ambitious. Over the six years he served in the post, he pushed through wide-ranging reforms, from encouraging freedom of speech and improving the economy, to building better foreign relations. He also did much to strengthen Russia's reputation abroad, particularly with his involvement in ending the Cold War. His eventual resignation in 1991 marked the end of the Soviet Union.

▶ Mikhail Gorbachev becomes the first president of the Soviet Union.

MARCH

12

1925

FATHER OF MODERN CHINA, SUN YAT-SEN, DIES

Also known as Sun Zhongshan, Sun Yat-sen was the founder of China's Kuomintang (Nationalist Party) and was the first president of the Republic of China. When the news of his death was reported in the *South China Morning Post* a day later, the newspaper noted: 'Without him China will seem for a time "the play without Hamlet".' Sun was born to a farming family in Xiangshan, Guangdong. After time spent living in Hawaii and studying in Hong Kong, he founded the revolutionary Revive China Society and tried, unsuccessfully, to incite revolution in 1895 after China's

defeat in the Sino-Japanese War. After many years spent in exile abroad, and following the successful Wuchang Uprising of 1911, led by Huang Xing, Sun returned to China and began his provisional leadership. He was reported to have died of cancer of the liver, or possibly of the gallbladder, aged 58.

▼ Two soldiers greeting the President of the Chinese Republic, Sun Yat-sen, in Nanking, China, in 1911.

MARCH
13
2013

POPE FRANCIS IS ELECTED

Argentine Cardinal Jorge Mario Bergoglio became the first Latin American and the first Jesuit pontiff when he was elected by a papal conclave in 2013. The 76-year-old replaced an ageing Benedict XVI, who had resigned the month before, saying he was no longer strong enough to lead the church.

Bergoglio chose Francis as his papal name in honour of St Francis of Assisi, the 13th-century Italian reformer and patron saint of animals. He later explained that he had chosen the name because Brazilian Cardinal Cláudio Hummes had told him, "Don't forget the poor." "Immediately I thought of St Francis of Assisi," Pope Francis said;

> ❝ Francis was a man of peace, a man of poverty, a man who loved and protected creation. ❞

MARCH
14
1995

LEADER OF THE DISABILITY RIGHTS MOVEMENT DIES

When Ed Roberts attended the University of California, Berkeley, in 1962, he became the school's first severely disabled student. He had to live in the campus hospital so he could use his iron lung at night. Roberts was a quadriplegic who was paralysed from the neck down, with motion in just one finger. He went on to earn two degrees, teach political science at the university and found the Center for Independent Living in 1972. The centre helped to solve the day-to-day problems of people with disabilities, such as modifying cars to enable them to drive.

Roberts raised public awareness and changed perceptions about people with disabilities.

During his life, Roberts travelled the world to raise public awareness and change perceptions about people with disabilities, arguing for independent living. He was behind successful campaigns that demanded better access to public transport and helped to set up the World Institute on Disability.

MARCH

15
4 BCE

JULIUS CAESAR IS ASSASSINATED ON THE IDES OF MARCH

At the time of his death, Gaius Julius Caesar enjoyed unparalleled power; he ruled as 'perpetual dictator', and was treated like a king, with statues of him installed in every Roman temple. Senators could see the republican system crumbling before their eyes, and soon an assassination plot emerged. A planned senate meeting was chosen as the occasion for the murder, at the Theatre of Pompey, a few days before Caesar planned to leave Rome for a military campaign. Caesar's approximately 60 assassins included Gaius Cassius Longinus, Marcus Junius Brutus and Decimus Junius Brutus Albinus. The meeting had only just begun when the attackers pulled Caesar's toga from his neck and then started stabbing him with daggers they had concealed in their clothes. It is believed his last words were in Greek: '*Kai su teknon.*' meaning 'You too, my child.' He was thought to be addressing Marcus Brutus, whom he had favoured and trusted deeply. The assassin's mother was Caesar's mistress, leading to rumours that Brutus might have been the ruler's illegitimate son.

MARCH

16
37 CE

ROMAN EMPEROR TIBERIUS DIES Despite Tiberius' 23-year rule and his improvements to Rome's finances and civil service, by the time of his death he had become unpopular.

MARCH
17
1997

GUYANA'S FIRST FEMALE PM IS ELECTED Janet Jagan fought for independence from British rule and established Guyana's People's Progressive Party.

MARCH
18
1314

LAST GRAND MASTER OF THE KNIGHTS TEMPLAR IS KILLED After a campaign led by King Philip IV of France, Jacques De Molay was charged and burned at the stake.

MARCH
19
2006

REVEREND SHUTTLESWORTH GIVES HIS FINAL SERMON The 84-year-old civil rights activist gave his final sermon at the Greater New Light Baptist Church, Cincinnati.

MARCH
20
1852

BESTSELLER *UNCLE TOM'S CABIN* IS PUBLISHED Harriet Beecher Stowe's damning portrayal of the slave trade helped fuel the anti-slavery movement.

MARCH
21
1282

DAFYDD AP GRUFFYDD ATTACKS HAWARDEN CASTLE The attack in North Wales was the start of the Second Welsh War for independence from England.

MARCH
22
1980

ANIMAL RIGHTS ACTIVISTS FOUND PETA Ingrid Newkirk and Alex Pacheco's organisation later became a forceful national movement after a case in a Maryland research facility.

FOUNDING FATHER PATRICK HENRY GIVES HIS 'LIBERTY OR DEATH' SPEECH

In front of 120 delegates gathered in Richmond's St John's Church in Virginia for the Second Virginia Convention, Patrick Henry changed the course of American history with a speech that left the audience 'subdued and captivated', according to reports of the day. The meeting, which was attended by the likes of George Washington and Thomas Jefferson, was to discuss how the colony would negotiate with the British Crown. Henry was a well-respected lawyer, talented public speaker and staunch opponent of the British tax system. While some delegates were still holding out for peace, it was obvious to many, Henry included, that war was on the horizon – British troops were mobilising across the colonies in readiness – and he was determined to convince his fellow delegates to move toward a defensive stance.

Henry put forward a resolution proposing that the counties of Virginia raise a militia. When he took the floor in Richmond, Henry spoke animatedly about the Crown's refusal to acknowledge the colony's petitions and the animosity of armed British troops on American shores. The speech climaxed when he held his hands together as if in shackles and raised them to the heavens, proclaiming: "I know not what course others may take; but as for me, give me liberty," and then, grasping an ivory letter opener and pretending to stab himself in the chest, "or give me death!" His speech had the desired impact. The resolution passed by only a few votes and Henry was charged with organising the militia ready for combat. Some of the ragtag army embroidered 'Liberty or Death' onto their shirts.

◀ Print showing Patrick Henry making his 'Liberty or Death' speech in Virginia Assembly.

MARCH
24
1953

QUEEN MARY DIES IN HER SLEEP

When a fourth and final bulletin was posted outside Marlborough House in London on a corrugated iron screen regarding Queen Mary's health, the crowd pressed forward to read it. Women wept and men removed their hats at the news that the hugely popular queen, grandmother to Queen Elizabeth II, had passed away in her sleep. Mary was the wife of King George V and mother to Edward VIII – who famously abdicated the throne to marry American divorcee Wallis Simpson against his mother's advice – and his successor George VI. She had a strong sense of royal duty and patriotism that buoyed the British people through two world wars. She died three months before her granddaughter's coronation.

MARCH
25
1199

KING RICHARD I IS WOUNDED WHILE FIGHTING IN FRANCE

It was the fatal wound that brought down King Richard I, also known as *Cœur-de-Lion* or 'Lionheart', the King of England who barely spent any time in his domain, and instead spent his ten-year reign fighting the Crusades abroad. The French-speaking king earned his nickname for his prowess on the battlefield – he led rebellions against his own father, Henry II, and overpowered the mighty Muslim leader Saladin during the Third Crusade. But he could not stay away from a good fight, and it was during the siege of the castle of Châlus-Chabrol against the viscounts of Limoges that he was struck by a crossbow bolt. He died from his wound on 6th April. Richard had no heir and the throne passed to his brother John.

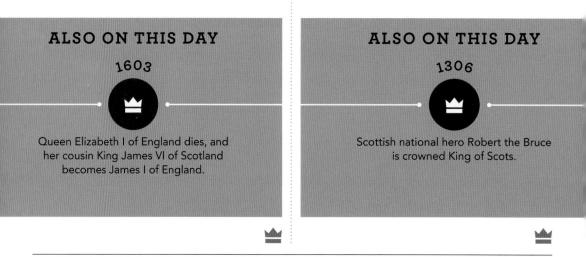

ALSO ON THIS DAY

1603

Queen Elizabeth I of England dies, and her cousin King James VI of Scotland becomes James I of England.

ALSO ON THIS DAY

1306

Scottish national hero Robert the Bruce is crowned King of Scots.

MARCH

26

1830

JOSEPH SMITH JR'S
BOOK OF MORMON IS PUBLISHED

Joseph Smith said he was visited by an angel named Moroni in 1823. The angel told him about an ancient record of prophetic writings by people who lived in North America in antiquity, but warned that he must obey a set of commandments before he would be eligible to read it. Four years later, Smith said that he found the Golden Plates buried on Cumorah Hill in New York State. He translated the contents into English and found eleven men to witness the plates and sign statements attesting to the fact. The translation was published as *The Book of Mormon: An Account Written by the Hand of Mormon upon Plates Taken from the Plates of Nephi*. It became one of the founding documents of the Latter Day Saints movement and a sacred text of the Mormon religion.

Joseph Smith translated the Golden Plates buried on Cumorah Hill into English and they were published later as *The Book of Mormon*.

▲ The angel Moroni delivering the plates of *The Book of Mormon* to Joseph Smith in New York, 1827.

MARCH

27

1886

APACHE LEADER GERONIMO SURRENDERS TO AMERICAN FORCES

When Geronimo surrendered at Cañón de Los Embudos in Sonora, Mexico, it had been ten months since the Bedonkohe Apache leader of the Chiricahua had fled the San Carlos reservation in May 1885, with 35 other men, 8 boys and 101 women. The tribe, who inhabited the area that is now New Mexico and Arizona, faced wars on two fronts: against the Spaniards and the North Americans. Geronimo had proved himself a brave and fearless warrior against the Mexicans and now outsmarted the Americans by escaping yet again, and evading capture for another five months. Travelling over 1,645 miles (2,650 km), he led more than 5,000 soldiers on a wild goose chase. In 1886 he was forced to surrender once again, and was exiled to Florida and put to hard labour.

▼ Geronimo (in the centre, to the right of the horse) stands with his warriors after surrendering to American forces in the Sierra Madre Mountains of Mexico, 27th March, 1886.

28
1760

ENGLISH ABOLITIONIST THOMAS CLARKSON IS BORN

While at Cambridge University, Thomas Clarkson won an essay competition on the subject of whether it was lawful to make someone a slave against their will. The widely read essay was published in 1786, and its argument became the basis of Clarkson's work for the rest of his life. Together with Granville Sharp, Clarkson formed the Committee for the Abolition of the African Slave Trade to try and persuade MP William Wilberforce to champion the abolitionist cause in Parliament. Clarkson was charged with gathering evidence of the slave trade from British ports and recording first-hand accounts. Thanks in large part to his efforts, slavery was abolished across the British Empire in 1807. Clarkson would not let up, working tirelessly to see that all British slaves were granted their freedom by the Slavery Abolition Act of 1833.

> **Thanks in large part to Clarkson's efforts, slavery was abolished across the British Empire in 1807.**

29
1857

MANGAL PANDEY MUTINIES AGAINST THE EAST INDIA COMPANY

Mangal Pandey was a soldier (sepoy) in the East India Company's army. He was ambitious, but as a member of the 6th Company of the 34th Bengal Native Infantry and a staunch Hindu Brahmin he was conflicted. Matters came to a head with the introduction of the Enfield rifle, which required the solder to bite off the ends of cartridges greased with cow or pig lard. This went against both Hindu and Muslim beliefs and led to unrest in the ranks. Pandey incited others to rise up against the British, and attacked two officers, before trying to end his own life. He was arrested, tried and executed on 8th April. Pandey's actions set in motion a larger revolt that took place in May that year.

ALSO ON THIS DAY

1974

Chinese farmers accidentally discover the Terracotta Army, part of a vast necropolis created in the 3rd century BCE for the first emperor of China.

MARCH

30

1981

PRESIDENT RONALD REAGAN IS SHOT

President Ronald Reagan had only been in office for 69 days when John Hinckley shot him as he left the Washington Hilton Hotel after addressing a union convention. Six shots rang out before Reagan was bundled into a limousine by secret service agents and driven to George Washington University Hospital, where he underwent surgery. Reagan had been struck by one ricocheting bullet, breaking a rib and puncturing a lung, but he survived to tell the tale. White House press secretary James Brady was also shot, as were a secret service official and a Washington policeman. Hinckley was found not guilty of his crimes by reason of insanity and was committed to hospital. Reagan's popularity soared in the wake of the incident, and four years later he went on to win a second term in office by a considerable margin.

▼ President Reagan waving to crowds before he was shot in an assassination attempt, in Washington, DC.

THE DALAI LAMA FLEES CHINA AND IS GRANTED POLITICAL ASYLUM IN INDIA

China considered Tibet to be its territory and had been waging a guerrilla war there for years against Tibetan rebels. When the 14th Dalai Lama was invited by the Chinese general Zhang Chenwu to watch a performance by a dance troupe at the Chinese military headquarters, the Tibetans were suspicious. Fearful he might be arrested or even killed, on 17th March, 1959, the 23-year-old leader disguised himself as a soldier and slipped through the crowds outside his palace in Lhasa,

accompanied by 20 officials and his family. The group's perilous journey included crossing the Brahmaputra river, 460 metres (500 yards) wide, and for two weeks his whereabouts remained unknown. On 31st March he crossed the Indian border at the Khenzimana Pass and found sanctuary at the Towang Monastery. He later settled in Dharamsala after being offered asylum. His departure led to an exile of 80,000 Tibetans.

▼ The Dalai Lama (fourth from left) flees from Tibet to India across the Himalayas. He is pictured here with his Khamba warrior guards during the journey.

CHAPTER

4

April

APRIL

1

528

BABY GIRL NAMED MALE HEIR OF CHINA

Hu Chonghua, Empress Dowager Ling, was the mother of Yuan Xu, who became China's Northern Wei Emperor Xiaoming. He took on the role when his father died suddenly, but because Yuan Xu was only six, his mother had *de facto* control of the imperial court. Many people resented the powerful influence she had, even her son. When Yuan Xu was 18, he tried to take power away from his mother and her advisors but was murdered in the process, on 31st March, 528. The following day Empress Dowager Ling announced that Yuan Xu's infant son was the new emperor (though the baby was, in fact, a girl). When this tactic failed, she then declared Yuan Xu's brother was actually the heir. Her efforts to retain a tight grip on imperial matters failed a few months later when she and the baby girl were drowned in the Yellow River.

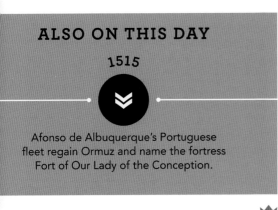

ALSO ON THIS DAY

1515

Afonso de Albuquerque's Portuguese fleet regain Ormuz and name the fortress Fort of Our Lady of the Conception.

APRIL

2

1851

SIAM'S PRINCE MONGKUT IS CROWNED RAMA IV

Prince Mongkut has become immortalised in *Anna and the King of Siam*, Margaret Landon's 1944 fictionalised account of Anna Leonowens' time spent as a teacher to the Siamese court in the late 19th century (which later gave rise to the musical *The King and I*), but Rama IV's real-life appointment of Leonowens as a Western teacher to his wives and children was central to his forward-thinking reign. He embraced Western commerce, securing treaties with Great Britain and the United States, while holding on to independence for the people of Siam (now Thailand). Mongkut's open-mindedness likely stemmed from his time spent as a monk and scholar before he became king. He studied Western science and languages, travelled around the country, unlike any ruler who came before him, and embraced American and French Christian missionaries.

> **Mongkut's open-mindedness likely stemmed from his time spent as a monk and scholar before he became king.**

APRIL

3

1948

PRESIDENT HARRY TRUMAN SIGNS OFF ON THE MARSHALL PLAN

President Harry Truman signed the Economic Assistance Act, known as the Marshall Plan and named after US Secretary of State George C. Marshall, was the post-war programme that aimed to help Europe's war-ravaged economy get back on track. The plan saw $13 billion in aid distributed to 17 European nations between 1948 and 1951. These direct grants and loans helped to reinvigorate agricultural, chemical, engineering and steel industries, significantly increasing the GNPs of the countries involved. The Marshall Plan had a huge impact on European economies, and the knock-on benefit for the US of a wider trade market. Truman had become president during World War II, after Franklin Roosevelt died, and was also responsible for the decision to drop atomic bombs on Japan and the negotiations to form NATO in the years that followed.

▼ Harry Truman signs the Marshall Plan into effect on 3rd April, 1948, in Washington, DC.

APRIL

4

1581

SIR FRANCIS DRAKE IS KNIGHTED BY QUEEN ELIZABETH I

Queen Elizabeth I had commissioned Sir Francis Drake to sail from England across the Atlantic and into the Pacific Ocean with the sole purpose of disrupting shipping and raiding Spanish settlements on what is now the Californian coast. When he arrived home after years at sea, he had completed the first English circumnavigation of the world. Of the five ships he set off with, only the *Pelican* remained. It was renamed the *Golden Hind* en route in honour of Drake's patron, Sir

Christopher Hatton, whose crest was a female red deer, and it was aboard this vessel that Elizabeth knighted her most intrepid sailor. In the years that followed, Drake was made a vice admiral, commanding the English fleet that defeated the Spanish Armada in 1588.

▼ Sir Francis Drake is knighted by Queen Elizabeth I while aboard the *Golden Hind*.

APRIL

5

1977

JUDITH HEUMANN LEADS SAN FRANCISCO'S DISABILITY RIGHTS SIT-IN

At 26 days, the 504 Sit-in remains the longest non-violent occupation of a US federal building in history. More than 100 disability rights activists were pushing for Secretary of Health, Education and Welfare, Joseph Califano, to sign binding regulations related to Section 504 of the Rehabilitation Act (1973) that would inform other agencies on how to implement the mandated integration of people with disabilities into mainstream institutions. As the protest gathered momentum and national press attention, 14 occupiers were chosen to go to Washington, DC, to try and force a meeting with Califano. Judith Heumann was one of them. At one point she gave a powerful speech:

> " I can tell you that every time you raise issues of 'separate but equal', the outrage of disabled individuals across this country is going to continue. It is going to be ignited. There will be more takeovers of buildings until finally maybe you begin to understand our position. "

Their efforts were successful. Regulations were signed on 28th April. Heumann went on to become an internationally recognised leader in disability rights. From 2010 to 2017 she was the first Special Advisor for International Disability Rights at the US Department of State.

◀ US Ambassador to Japan Caroline Kennedy welcomes Special Advisor for International Disability Rights Judith Heumann to Tokyo, Japan, on 4th December, 2014.

FLAVIUS STILICHO'S ARMY WINS THE BATTLE OF POLLENTIA

At a time when the Roman Empire had been split in two, Flavius Stilicho was father-in-law to the child Western Emperor Honorius. As the ten-year-old's army commander, he essentially ruled the roost, and managed to keep the empire intact, until the Visigoths came along. Their king, Alaric, had led a rampage through the Eastern Empire and now set his sights on the West. Alaric's onslaught ended at the Battle of Pollentia (modern-day Pollenzo, Italy), where Stilicho made the tactical decision to attack Alaric's camp on Easter Sunday – the Visigoths followed a version of Christianity that meant they would be holding services on that day. The plan paid off: the Visigoths were caught off guard and, though the slaughter was immense on both sides, Alaric's forces never recovered and the Goths were forced to flee southward, abandoning their women, children and treasure.

> **Stilicho made the tactical decision to attack Alaric's camp on Easter Sunday.**

JESUS IS CRUCIFIED BY ROMAN TROOPS IN JERUSALEM

After being questioned by a group of Jewish officials, preacher Jesus Christ was tried by Roman governor Pontius Pilate on a charge of treason. Though the governor thought a flogging would be sufficient punishment for Jesus's crimes, the crowd demanded an execution. Jesus was whipped and forced to carry a wooden cross through the streets to Calvary or Golgotha, where he was stripped and nailed to the cross with a sign placed above his head that read 'King of the Jews'. After some hours, his body was stabbed to make sure he was dead before he was cut down. In the Christian faith, Jesus is believed to be the Son of God and the Messiah. As a historical figure, he is considered to be one of the most influential people of all time.

Though the exact date of the Crucifixion is not known, the evidence suggests it was on a Friday, in spring, on a full moon, on either the first day of Passover or the eve of Passover, between 25 and 35 CE. Other widely accepted dates are 3rd April, 33 CE; 6th April, 30 CE and 18th March, 29 CE.

APRIL

8

563

GAUTAMA BUDDHA'S BIRTHDAY

Modern scholars believe Gautama Buddha lived in India between 563 and 483 BCE, in the area that borders present-day Nepal and India. The earliest existing record of the founder of Buddhism's life, the *Tripitaka*, states that he was known as Prince Siddhartha, and was born to King Suddhodana of the Sakya people and Queen Mahamaya, who reportedly gave birth to him in a park called Lumbini – now a pilgrimage site for Buddhists. Buddha's fate was predicted at his birth. The Brahmans, the highest-ranking members of Hindu society – prophesied that the baby boy would become either a great ruler or an enlightened teacher, so his father kept him inside the confines of the palace complex, in the hope he would not become interested in a religious way of life. When he was 29, he ventured further and further from the palace, until he set out for the final time in search of *nirvana*, the highest level of enlightenment.

▼ A golden statue of Buddha.

9

1768

JOHN HANCOCK REBUFFS BRITISH CUSTOMS AGENTS

When the British established the American Board of Commissioners in 1767, with the hope of collecting more customs taxes from importers to American soil, they had not anticipated the likes of John Hancock, one of the wealthiest men in Massachusetts. When customs agents boarded his vessel, *Lydia*, Hancock demanded they produce search warrants before going below decks. When they failed to do so, Hancock insisted they leave. A month later, when they tried to search another of his ships, the *Liberty*, Hancock's captain bribed the officials. This set in motion the Liberty Affair, in which the British seized the ship, causing a colonist mob to retaliate by burning British port collector Joseph Harrison's own ship. The customs officials soon fled the city, rightly fearing the further civil unrest that was to come. Hancock would go on to be the first person to sign the Declaration of Independence in 1776.

Hancock demanded they produce search warrants before going below decks.

10

1919

MEXICAN REVOLUTION LEADER IS AMBUSHED AND KILLED

After presidential candidate Francisco Madero lost the election to Mexico's tyrannical leader Porfirio Díaz, Madero's call to revolution spread to the provinces, and the country's peasants answered loudly. Emiliano Zapata was from the southern state of Morelos and soon became a legendary figure, leading a peasant army whose members called themselves Zapatistas. By 1914, together with the north's Francisco 'Pancho' Villa and his followers, they had occupied Mexico City and overthrown the sitting president. Neither Zapata nor Villa was interested in running a government, and Zapata soon returned home, where he continued to seize land from rich estate owners and distribute it to peasants. When Venustiano Carranza was elected president in 1917, he realised the influence Zapata had over the south, an area rich in natural resources, and decided to have him killed. Colonel Jesús Guajardo arranged a meeting with Zapata, telling him he was going to defect from the federal army, but when the revolutionary arrived at the hacienda, a trumpet sounded his arrival, and the colonel's troops fired on him and his men. To let the world know Zapata was no more, the officers took the corpse to the local police station and released photographs.

APRIL

11

1241

BATU KHAN DEFEATS KING BÉLA IV OF HUNGARY

At the time of the Battle of Mohi, the Hungarian army was known for having the most skilled cavalry in Europe – but then came the Mongols. The three-pronged assault took place south-west of the Sajo River with Genghis Khan's grandson, Batu Khan, leading the charge. After advancing on Pest, the Mongols retreated east of the city with Béla's forces hot on their tails. The two armies made camps on opposite sides of the river by the main bridge crossing, but Mongol general Subedei directed two groups to scout out alternative crossings north and south from there.

Béla had grown unpopular, and as a result a number of nobles declined to pledge their military might to their king. Despite this, the Hungarian troops outnumbered the Mongolians, and when a third of the Mongolian army advanced across the bridge towards them, Béla must have had victory in his sights. But he had not accounted for the additional Mongolians who had found alternative crossings and soon surrounded his encampment on all sides. The Mongolian victory ensured their control over Eastern Europe.

APRIL

12

2015

HILLARY CLINTON RUNS FOR PRESIDENT It was Clinton's second attempt, after losing out to Barack Obama in 2008.

APRIL

13

1919

EUGENE VICTOR DEBS IS IMPRISONED After his speech against America's involvement in World War I and the draft, activist Debs was sentenced to ten years in prison.

APRIL

14

1865

PRESIDENT ABRAHAM LINCOLN IS ASSASSINATED Lincoln was the first American president to be assassinated. He was shot at Ford's Theater in Washington.

APRIL

15

1755

SAMUEL JOHNSON'S DICTIONARY IS PUBLISHED *A Dictionary of the English Language* was the most widely used in Britain for 150 years.

APRIL

16

1869

FIRST AFRICAN AMERICAN FOREIGN DIPLOMAT Activist and educator Ebenezer Bassett made history when he became American Minister Resident to Haiti.

APRIL

17

1982

CANADA BECOMES AN INDEPENDENT NATION Queen Elizabeth II signed the Proclamation of the Constitution Act, granting Canada full independence from Britain.

APRIL

18

1916

EDITH WHARTON RECEIVES FRANCE'S HIGHEST AWARD The novelist was appointed Chevalier of the Legion of Honor for her refugee aid work during World War I.

APRIL

19

1782

JOHN ADAMS ESTABLISHES THE FIRST AMERICAN EMBASSY

The Netherlands was the first country to recognise the United States as a distinct country.

Well known for being the second president of the United States, John Adams was also the country's first ambassador. As 'minister plenipotentiary' to the Dutch Republic, he was received by the country's States General in the Hague and presented his credentials. The Netherlands was the first country to recognise the United States as a distinct country, not just a colony of the British. Adams' own house in the Hague was the first American embassy, but a month later he moved into the US's first diplomatic building, the Hôtel des Etats-Unis. The future president was there to network with the elite of the continent's biggest financial market and secure support for the republic's Revolutionary War. Later that year he successfully negotiated and signed the Treaty of Amity and Commerce with the Netherlands, securing a trade deal and a vast loan for the fledgling nation.

APRIL

20

1653

OLIVER CROMWELL DISSOLVES THE RUMP PARLIAMENT

During England's Civil War, Puritan Cromwell led the New Model Army for the Parliamentarians, resulting in the surrender of King Charles I. In 1648 the military took over, purging Parliament by arresting and excluding those members who were unlikely to support a forceful punishment of the king. What remained was a 'rump' of just 200 members. After the king's subsequent trial and beheading, the Rump Parliament passed laws abolishing the monarchy and the House of Lords. But the Rump did not live up to Cromwell's expectations – its members did not trust Cromwell's powerful army and refused to push through the reformist legislation he wanted. So the *de facto* ruler led an armed force into the Commons chamber and forced it to dissolve, saying:

" You have sat too long for any good you have been doing lately. In the name of God, go! "

APRIL
21
1876

STOYAN ZAIMOV LEADS BULGARIA'S APRIL UPRISING

The atrocities fuelled demands for reform of the Ottoman Empire.

Stoyan Zaimov led one of five revolutionary districts across Bulgaria in the revolutionary insurrection against Ottoman Imperial rule. He worked as a teacher and lived in Romania, where he founded the Giurgiu Revolutionary Committee, which made preparations for the uprising. He returned to his native Bulgaria at the start of 1876, and in April, after two Ottoman police officers were shot by a local rebel committee in Koprivshtitsa, the revolution started two weeks earlier than planned. The Ottoman army fought back with full force – thousands of civilians were slaughtered and by mid-May the uprising was over. Zaimov was sentenced to death, but was released shortly after as a result of the 1878 Treaty of San Stefano, following the Russo-Turkish War. Though the revolution was ultimately unsuccessful, the atrocities inflicted on the Bulgarian rebels caused an international outcry and fuelled demands for reform of the Ottoman Empire.

APRIL
22
1951

MACARTHUR COMES HOME

It was one of the biggest ticker-tape parades ever held in New York City. General Douglas MacArthur, who was by then one of the most famous military leaders in the world, having led the Allied forces during World War II, was taking a tour of the United States. The general had been fired on 11th April by President Truman after the two men disagreed about the Korean War. Though the general's strategies had prevented South Korea from succumbing to communist forces, he wanted to push further into North Korea. When Chinese forces joined the fray against the Americans, MacArthur wanted to retaliate by bombing the People's Republic of China, but Truman refused. The public was shocked to hear of the general's dismissal. When he arrived in New York, the parade to greet him stretched for 19 miles (30 km) – 7 million New Yorkers showed up to welcome their war hero home.

▶ Paper showers down on MacArthur during a parade in his honour in New York City. This view is looking south on Lafayette Street in lower Manhattan.

APRIL

23

1702

QUEEN ANNE IS CROWNED

Queen Anne's coronation saw her become Queen of England, Scotland, Ireland and (theoretically) France. Anne inherited the throne after the death of her sister Queen Mary II and brother-in-law King William III (they had no children). The 37-year-old queen suffered from rheumatism, so she was unable to walk to her own coronation. Instead she was carried to Westminster Abbey in an open chair, covered by a canopy, her 5.5-metre (6-yard) red velvet train trailing in her wake. Despite her ailments, multiple devastating miscarriages, the death of her 11-year-old son and heir, and her reported lack of intelligence, Anne was a popular queen among her subjects, and oversaw the Act of Union in 1707 that unified England and Scotland, making her the first sovereign of Great Britain.

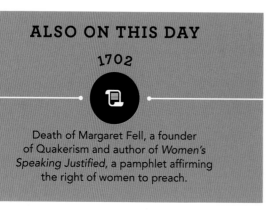

ALSO ON THIS DAY

1702

Death of Margaret Fell, a founder of Quakerism and author of *Women's Speaking Justified*, a pamphlet affirming the right of women to preach.

APRIL

24

1184 BCE

THE GREEKS ENTER TROY USING THE TROJAN HORSE

Contemporary knowledge of the Trojan war comes from Classical sources that vary in their telling – the date given here is one of many that have been proposed. The Bronze Age conflict between the Mycenaeans and the Trojans lasted for nearly 10 years, and is said to have begun when the Trojan prince Paris abducted Helen of Sparta (her brother-in-law was Agamemnon, king of Mycenae). The Mycenaeans gathered the greatest warriors they could find, including Greek heroes Odysseus and Achilles, and sailed across the Aegean Sea to Troy, where the lengthy war ensued. According to legend, the tide turned when Odysseus and a group of soldiers hid inside a wooden horse, which they left at the city's gates. Intrigued, the Trojans pulled it inside, only to be ambushed by the warriors lurking within, who took down Troy from the inside. According to the Greek poet Homer, who wrote about these events several centuries later, it took Odysseus ten years to make his journey home to Ithaca.

25

1974

GENERAL ANTÓNIO DE SPÍNOLA SEIZES CONTROL OF PORTUGAL

Known as the Carnation Revolution, this was the day that ended nearly 50 years of dictatorship by the Estado Novo (New State) government under António de Oliveira Salazar and his successor Marcelo Caetano. António de Spínola had served as governor and commander-in-chief of the army in Portuguese Guinea as well as deputy armed forces minister, but he had become disillusioned with the 13-year war Portugal had been fighting to retain its colonies. After army rebels drove their tanks into Lisbon, seized control of the airport and stormed the barracks where Prime Minister Caetano had taken refuge, it was Spínola to whom Caetano insisted on surrendering. The new regime, with Spínola as interim president, started the process of decolonisation almost immediately, with Guinea-Bissau, the Cape Verde Islands, Mozambique, São Tomé and Principe, and Angola all gaining independence. There was also a push to nationalise Portugal's economy and release hundreds of political prisoners.

Caetano insisted on surrending to Spínola.

▲ A few days after Portugal is seized, General António de Spínola is pictured among his captains, generals, corporals and colonels.

APRIL

26

1478

LORENZO AND GIULIANO DE' MEDICI ARE ATTACKED IN FLORENCE CATHEDRAL

It was High Mass at Florence's Duomo and thousands of worshippers had gathered to celebrate Easter Sunday. Among them were the Medici brothers, the most powerful men in Florence; Francesco de' Pazzi, from the Tuscan nobility; and Francesco Salviati. The Pazzi and Salviati families were plotting to usurp the Medicis as rulers of the Florentine Republic. When the cardinal raised the Sacred Host, the cathedral bells rang out and the men made their move towards the brothers, killing Giuliano by stabbing him repeatedly with a knife. They also attacked Lorenzo, but he managed to escape. The public was enraged by the Pazzi Conspiracy and hunted down the collaborators in a bloody witch hunt that saw 200 Pazzi family members lose their lives.

> ## The public was enraged and hunted down the collaborators in a bloody witch hunt.

▶ Statue of Lorenzo de' Medici in the Uffizi Gallery, Florence, Italy.

APRIL

1961

SIERRA LEONE ELECTS ITS FIRST PM

Before he became the first prime minister of an independent Sierra Leone, Milton Margai was a doctor who had attended King's College Medical School in Newcastle upon Tyne, England. He returned to his home country of Sierra Leone to open a village dispensary, and then worked across the country as a surgeon and obstetrician. Before his political career began, he started a campaign to improve childcare provisions and raise literacy standards. As the leader of the majority Sierra Leone People's Party, he became chief minister in 1954, and subsequently prime minister. The party promoted nationalism, albeit moderately, and Margai was at the forefront of petitioning for independence talks in London, which took place in 1960. Less than a year later, Margai received the formal documents of sovereignty from Britain's Duke of Kent at a celebration held in the Freetown National Stadium.

Margai was at the forefront of petitioning for independence talks in London, which took place in 1960.

APRIL

1789

SAILORS ARE SET ADRIFT AFTER THE MUTINY ON THE *BOUNTY*

The sailors decided that they would rather spend their lives on a tropical island than head back to Britain.

As if life as an 18th-century sailor were not hard enough, Lieutenant Bligh and the non-rebellious members of his crew had to face the perilous Pacific waters aboard a 7-metre (23-foot) open boat after half the ship's company, led by Fletcher Christian, decided that they would rather spend their lives on a tropical island than head back to Britain. Cast adrift near Tonga, their chances did not look good. Bligh and the 18-strong crew had only a sextant and a pocket watch to navigate by – they lacked the charts and marine chronometer that they were accustomed to using – and only a small supply of food and water. It was Bligh's leadership and expert seamanship that enabled the men to survive against the odds. After a 47-day journey, travelling over 3,500 nautical miles (6,500 km), all but one of the crew (who was killed when they stopped for supplies on the island of Tofua) arrived in the colonial outpost of the Dutch East Indies.

APRIL

29

1770

CAPTAIN JAMES COOK ARRIVES IN BOTANY BAY, AUSTRALIA

Captain James Cook worked hard to earn his place at the helm of HMS *Endeavour*, the Royal Navy coal ship that would carry him and his fellow sailors to the southern hemisphere in search of the southern continent. Born in a small Yorkshire village, the son of a farmer, Cook made a name for himself in the Royal Navy, serving in North America. His leadership skills and expertise in surveying and charting coastal waters made him the ideal commander for the expedition that set off in 1769 and made landfall at what Cook named Botany Bay the following year. After returning home to Britain, Cook would make further pioneering trips to the Antarctic coast and New Zealand, and then to Hawaii after a failed search to find the Northwest Passage linking the Atlantic and Pacific oceans.

▲ Coloured halftone of Captain James Cook taking possession of Australia for King George III.

APRIL

30

1789

GEORGE WASHINGTON TAKES THE OATH OF OFFICE

Even bad weather could not prevent America's first president, George Washington, taking the oath of office, although it did delay proceedings by over a month. After winning the election by 69 electoral votes on 6th April, Washington travelled to New York City, where the government was temporarily located, to be sworn in. The oath was administered by the New York Chancellor, Robert R. Livingston, on the second-floor balcony of Federal Hall – crowds had gathered below to witness history in the making. After the ceremony was concluded, Washington and the other members of Congress went into the Senate chamber where the new president delivered his inaugural address.

> 66 **I hope I shall possess firmness and virtue enough to maintain what I consider the most enviable of all titles, the character of an honest man.** 99
>
> GEORGE WASHINGTON

▼ This 1860 engraving by John Rogers depicts George Washington at his swearing-in ceremony at New York's Federal Hall.

CHAPTER

5

May

PRESIDENT OBAMA ANNOUNCES THE DEATH OF OSAMA BIN LADEN

In a late-night broadcast to the American people, and the world, President Barack Obama announced that a US military and CIA operation had led to the location and assassination of al-Qaeda leader Osama bin Laden, who was killed after a raid on a complex in Pakistan where he had been living with his family. In a defining moment of Obama's presidency, he looked into the camera and said:

"Tonight, let us think back to the sense of unity that prevailed on 9/11. I know that it has at times frayed, yet today's achievement is a testament to the greatness of our country and the determination of the American people."

A US military and CIA operation had led to the assassination of the al-Qaeda leader.

▼ Barack Obama makes a televised statement from the White House about the death of Osama bin Laden.

MAY

2

1559

KNOX RETURNS TO LEAD THE PROTESTANT REFORMATION

In his day, John Knox was one of the most powerful preachers of the Christian gospel. He was born and raised near Edinburgh before studying theology at university and becoming a teacher to the sons of local noblemen. This was at a time when many Scots were becoming increasingly angry towards the Catholic church – it owned much of the land and claimed a substantial annual tax from the people. But Lutheran teachings were being smuggled into Scotland across the sea, and soon Knox was being influenced by the writings of Frenchman Thomas Guilliame and Scottish preacher George Wishart, for whom he became a bodyguard. He travelled to England to take part in the Reformation there, and even preached before the Protestant King Edward VI, but the burden of being a preacher was immense – when Catholic Mary I ascended to the English throne in 1553 he fled to Europe, preaching in Frankfurt and Geneva. A year after he returned from his exile, the Scottish Parliament passed laws that abolished the Catholic Mass and eroded the Pope's power.

MAY

3

1481 & 1534

MOTHER JUANA DE LA CRUZ IS BORN AND DIES As abbess at Santa María de la Cruz, near Madrid, she gave spiritual guidance to nobles and religious leaders.

MAY

4

1910

SIR WILFRED LAURIER SIGNS THE NAVAL SERVICE BILL The Canadian Premier had promised to develop Canada's armed forces. The bill created the Royal Canadian Navy.

MAY

5

1260

KUBLAI KHAN RULES THE MONGOL EMPIRE Genghis Khan's grandson was the first Mongol to rule over China, founding the Yuan Dynasty.

MAY

6

1910

GEORGE V BECOMES KING OF THE UNITED KINGDOM He later renamed his dynasty the House of Windsor due to the public's anti-German view during World War I.

MAY

7

1664

LOUIS XIV INAUGURATES THE PALACE OF VERSAILLES The French king held a week-long fete to mark the start of the first building campaign to expand the palace grounds.

MAY

8

1753

PRIEST DON MIGUEL HIDALGO IS BORN The Roman Catholic priest would go on to lead the Hidalgo Revolt, which started the Mexican War of Independence in 1810.

MAY

9

1980

POLITICAL ACTIVIST KATE MOLALE DIES The South African former Secretary General of the Sophiatown branch of the African National Congress was killed in a car accident.

MAY

10

1924

J. EDGAR HOOVER BECOMES DIRECTOR OF THE FBI

The Bureau of Investigation, which later became the FBI in 1935, was run by Hoover for 48 years. The former assistant to the attorney general was just 29 when he took on the role of director at America's federal law enforcement organisation. He made important institutional changes, setting hiring standards and training requirements for special agents, and introduced professional forensic protocols and laboratories. Hoover's programme of espionage saw the FBI monitoring anyone who did not conform to the director's ideals and because of this, he held huge sway and influence over political leaders. A few years after Hoover's death, Congress passed the 1976 Crime Control Act which limited the FBI's directorship to a ten-year term.

ALSO ON THIS DAY

1872

Victoria Woodhull becomes the first woman to be nominated as an American presidential candidate, by the Equal Rights Party.

MAY

11

1812

SPENCER PERCEVAL KILLED IN THE HOUSE OF COMMONS

Spencer Perceval was a barrister and father of 13 who had swiftly risen up the ranks of the Conservative Party to take over from William Pitt the Younger as prime minister in 1809. He was a key proponent of the Slave Trade Act, banning the practice throughout the British Empire and helping to establish the West Africa Squadron, an anti-slavery naval force. As prime minister he had the support of the Prince Regent, after passing the Regency Bill of 1810 because of George III's ailing mental health. But he is most widely remembered for the fact that while arriving in the Commons on this Monday in May, he was shot in the heart by John Bellingham, a disgruntled commission agent and former East India Service employee who was trying to claim compensation from the government.

> **Perceval was shot in the heart by John Bellingham, a disgruntled commission agent and former East India Service employee.**

MAY

12

1789

WILBERFORCE ADDRESSES THE HOUSE OF COMMONS

66 **When I consider the magnitude of the subject which I am to bring before the House – a subject in which the interests, not of this country, nor of Europe alone, but of the whole world, and of posterity, are involved ... it is impossible for me not to feel both terrified and concerned at my own inadequacy to such a task.** 99

WILLIAM WILBERFORCE

British MP William Wilberforce was more than adequate – both in this speech, in which he laid bare the atrocities of the slave trade and put forward 12 propositions for its abolition, and in his wider efforts to dismantle this appalling industry. Despite losing his first abolition bill debate by 163 votes to 88, Wilberforce continued to introduce similar petitions and legislation for more than a decade, until the Abolition Act was passed in 1807.

MAY

13

1981

POPE JOHN PAUL II IS SHOT

Pope John Paul II's weekly drive in his chauffeured open-topped car through St Peter's Square in Rome, where he would bless the crowds who had gathered there, took a dark turn in 1981 when a man reached for his arm and then fired four shots directly at the pope. Two of these hit the pontiff; the other two hit two bystanders. The crowd pounced on the would-be assassin – Mehmet Ali Ağca, a wanted murderer and fascist who had escaped from a Turkish prison – while the pope was rushed to hospital for emergency surgery, which he survived.

John Paul II was head of the Catholic Church from 1978 to 2005, making him the second longest-serving pope in modern history. Though criticised by some for his conservative interpretations of the Church's teachings, he is credited with improving Catholicism's relationship with other faiths.

A man reached for his arm and then fired four shots directly at the pope.

▶ Bodyguards hold Pope John Paul II after he was shot by a Turkish extremist.

MAY

14

1643

FOUR-YEAR-OLD LOUIS XIV BECOMES KING OF FRANCE

The reign of Louis XIV, the 'Sun King,' lasted 72 years – the longest of any known European monarch. It was a period of radical change in France, with an explosion of art and literature, and the relocation of the royal court and government to the extravagant Palace of Versailles. It was from there that Louis wooed rebellious nobles with decadence and diversion, which helped him tighten his grip on France and its overseas colonies. But it all started when the four-year-old was crowned and his mother, Anne of Austria, became his sole regent. Together with Cardinal Jules Mazarin, she cemented her young son's power and arranged a strategic marriage with Marie-Thérèse, daughter of King Philip IV of Spain.

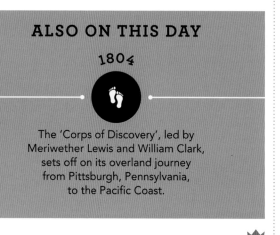

ALSO ON THIS DAY

1804

The 'Corps of Discovery', led by Meriwether Lewis and William Clark, sets off on its overland journey from Pittsburgh, Pennsylvania, to the Pacific Coast.

MAY

15

1957

EVANGELIST BILLY GRAHAM LAUNCHES HIS NEW YORK CRUSADE

Over 16 weeks, more than 2.3 million people attended 38-year-old Billy Graham's New York Crusade at Madison Square Garden. It was meant to last just six weeks. The Southern fundamentalist preacher opened to a crowd of 18,500, telling the congregation:

> " **Listen with your soul tonight; your heart also has ears.** "

The day after, the *New York Times* printed his entire sermon in full. By the time the four-month-long campaign was through, Graham was the most famous evangelist preacher in the United States. Having previously toured Europe, he would later travel to Australia, Africa and South America. He met with every post-World War II president, from Truman to Obama, and was a spiritual advisor to some of them.

MAY

16

1925

THE 'MOTHER OF HUBBLE' IS BORN

Nancy Roman was NASA's first chief of astronomy as well as the first woman to be employed at the agency in an executive position. Under her command, the origins of what would become the Hubble space telescope emerged. Known as the 'mother of Hubble', she began life as the daughter of a music teacher and geophysicist. As a child she set her sights on an astronomy career, and despite the many barriers facing women in the sciences, she progressed from Chicago's Yerkes Observatory to the US government's Naval Research Laboratory before securing the position at NASA six months after the agency opened. While she had been long-retired in 1990 when Hubble was finally launched, it was her approach to its development – a collaborative effort between astronomers and engineers – that led to the telescope's long-lasting success.

Nancy Roman was NASA's first chief of astronomy as well as the first woman to be employed at the agency in an executive position.

MAY

17

1805

MUHAMMAD ALI BECOMES OTTOMAN VICEROY OF EGYPT

Ali would continue to rule over Egypt until his death in 1849, but he had created a dynasty that would outlive him by more than a century.

After gaining the support of the general public, in particular the Albanian Ottomans whom Muhammad Ali had led against Napoleon's forces years earlier, the military commander's appointment as viceroy marked the start of a swift rise to power. Where previously the Ottomans had struggled to maintain control over the Mamluks, descendants of slave-warriors who had been brought to Egypt centuries before and wanted independence from the Ottoman Empire, Ali crushed his opponents, culminating in a brutal massacre in 1811 known as the Battle of the Citadel. He then set to work modernising the country, developing its industry and agriculture. Ali would continue to rule over Egypt until his death in 1849, but he had created a dynasty that would outlive him by more than a century.

MAY

18

1804

NAPOLEON'S FIRST REIGN AS EMPEROR BEGINS

As first consul of the Republic, Napoleon Bonaparte had once claimed that:

> **My natural heir is the French people.**

But by 1803 he was working towards cementing his position of power. His coronation on 2nd December, 1804 marked the adoption of his title as Emperor of the French, but it was a *Sénatus-consulte* (an act of the Senate), which the hand-picked Senate had adopted in May, that made his coronation possible.

An election was held in order to determine whether the public were amenable to his change in status. The results showed that 99.93 per cent of voters gave a positive response, but by then the elaborate plans for the coronation ceremony were already in motion, which suggests the results were doctored.

MAY

19

1536

ANNE BOLEYN IS EXECUTED

Anne Boleyn's hold over Henry VIII, and her refusal to be his mistress, ultimately led to establishment of the Church of England and the English Reformation. But Boleyn was not merely an attractive woman at court. Skilled in the art of diplomacy, she had served as a maid of honour in other European courts and to Henry's first wife. She would greet foreign dignitaries and engage with political leaders; most notably, she had a close relationship with Thomas Cromwell, Henry's chief minister. It was this power as Queen of England, coupled with her inability to produce a male heir, that led to her downfall. Boleyn and Cromwell clashed over financial issues and foreign policy, and it was Cromwell, among others, who investigated Boleyn and charged her with adultery, incest and conspiracy. Her trial took place just five days before her execution, which left Henry free (and single) to marry again.

It was Cromwell, among others, who investigated Boleyn and charged her with adultery, incest and conspiracy.

COUNT FOLKE BERNADOTTE IS APPOINTED UNITED NATIONS MEDIATOR IN PALESTINE

By July 1948, Swedish diplomat Bernadotte had managed to arrange a 30-day ceasefire between the Jewish and Arab sides fighting in the newly created state of Israel. He was a decorated hero of both world wars, but the count's future plans for the region were unpopular on both sides. Tragically, just four months after his appointment, Bernadotte was travelling through West Jerusalem on his way to a meeting when a car blocked his convoy at what appeared to be an army checkpoint. There were four men in the car, three of whom got out and started firing at Bernadotte's vehicle. He was shot six times and died from his injuries. Authorities suspected members of Lehi, a Jewish terrorist group, although no one was ever charged with the murder.

▼ Bernadotte and his wife, Estelle, are greeted by the United Nations Secretary General, Trygve Lie, at Laguardia Airport in New York City on 12th July, 1948.

MAY

21

1881

CIVIL WAR NURSE FOUNDS THE AMERICAN RED CROSS

Clara Barton's pioneering work began long before she lobbied for America to sign the Geneva Convention, which was established by the International Red Cross in Geneva, Switzerland. She had been a self-taught nurse on the battlefields of America's bloody Civil War. Realising that the front lines were lacking basic medical care and supplies, she obtained permission to travel with the Union army and administer care in field hospitals. But it was her travels in Europe, nursing the troops in the Franco-Prussian War of 1870, that inspired her true calling. Thanks to Barton, President Chester A. Arthur signed the Geneva Convention in 1882, and the American Red Cross was born. Under her influence, the treaty was extended to include providing aid to the victims of natural disasters.

ALSO ON THIS DAY

1927

Charles Lindbergh completes the first solo, non-stop transatlantic flight. Five years later, Amelia Earhart becomes the first woman to do the same.

MAY

22

334 BCE

ALEXANDER THE GREAT WINS THE BATTLE OF THE GRANICUS

Alexander decided to attack immediately, charging across the water.

When Alexander the Great of Macedonia arrived in the western-most reaches of the Persian empire, he was not alone. A 37,000-strong army composed of Macedonians and Greeks had followed the young king to modern-day Turkey to carry out his father's dream of putting the Persians in their place. King Philip had been assassinated two years earlier, passing the mantle to his 20-year-old son, who by then was an experienced cavalry commander. The two enemies faced each other from opposite banks of the Granicus River when Alexander decided to attack immediately, charging across the water when the Persians were least expecting it. He kept the upper hand, and the decisive battle, which saw just 100 Macedonian lives lost in comparison with 1,000 Persians, marked the first step in Alexander's conquest of Asia.

23

1940

TROTSKY SURVIVES AN ASSASSINATION ATTEMPT

Less than three months before the Russian revolutionary was assassinated on 20th August, 1940, under orders from Joseph Stalin, he had miraculously survived another attempt on his life. Leon Trotsky had been living in Mexico since being exiled from his homeland in 1929. He was at home with his wife and grandson at their house in Mexico City when a group of 20 members of the NKVD (the Soviet Union's People's Commissariat for Internal Affairs) tied up the armed guards outside and fired a rain of bullets on the house from the courtyard, before placing a bomb which failed to explode. The family crouched on the floor while the attack took place, and the only injury was to Trotsky's grandson's toe. One of the most influential Russians of the 20th century, Trotsky had endured far worse, including imprisonment and exile to Siberia for inciting revolution.

The family crouched on the ground while the attack took place, and the only injury was to Trotsky's grandson's toe.

24

1813

SIMÓN BOLÍVAR FREES VENEZUELAN TERRITORIES

The Admirable Campaign was a decisive military action and a key stage in liberating Venezuela.

Venezuelan Simón Bolívar received a broad education and was tutored in the 18th-century liberal ideas of John Locke, Voltaire and Jean-Jacques Rousseau. He went on to author two key political treatises that rallied the people of South America to join the independence movement. After Venezuela's first independence effort failed, he returned to his homeland to lead expeditionary forces against the Spanish. The Admirable Campaign was a decisive military action that freed the provinces of Mérida, Barinas, Trujillo and Caracas from Spanish rule and was one of the key stages in liberating Venezuela. Between 1819 and 1822, Bolívar went on to liberate New Granada and Quito. Later, he earned himself the title 'Liberator of Five Nations' when, together with José de San Martín, he helped to free Peru and the territory which later became Bolivia, named in his honour.

MAY

25

1961

KENNEDY SAYS THAT AMERICA WILL PUT A MAN ON THE MOON

It is undoubtedly one of John F. Kennedy presidency's defining legacies. In a speech to a joint session of Congress, which aired on TV and radio around the world, Kennedy said:

> " I believe that this nation should commit itself to achieving the goal, before this decade is out, of landing a man on the Moon and returning him safely to Earth. "

He was requesting $9 billion (£3,214 million at the time) from the federal budget to make it happen. The speech came a month after Russian cosmonaut Yuri Gagarin became the first man in space. America was losing the race and it was time to pick up the pace. The president's commitment paid off when on 21st July, 1969, six years after Kennedy's assassination, Neil Armstrong set foot on the Moon.

MAY

26

1940

ALLIED TROOPS EVACUATE FRANCE

In the early stages of World War II, German forces had pushed the Allied troops into an isolated pocket in Northern France – evacuation was the only option. Starting on this day, 'Operation Dynamo' saw 338,000 Allied troops safely reach English shores after escaping by ship from the French port of Dunkirk (Dunkerque). Initially, it was expected that only 45,000 men might be saved. It was the biggest evacuation in military history and ensured the future of Britain's army – a priceless asset in the years that followed. Prime Minister Churchill later delivered a speech to Parliament that spoke of the country's determination to defend itself, support its allies and 'outlive the menace of tyranny'.

> " We shall defend our island, whatever the cost may be, we shall fight on the beaches, we shall fight on the landing grounds, we shall fight in the fields and in the streets, we shall fight in the hills; we shall never surrender... "
>
> WINSTON CHURCHILL

MAY

27

1963

JOMO KENYATTA BECOMES THE FIRST PM OF KENYA

After years of struggle for independence, Jomo Kenyatta led the Kenya African National Union to victory in the country's first post-independence general election, taking 58 seats in comparison with the Kenya African Democratic Union's 28. Already in his 70s, he had been involved in politics since the late 1920s, travelling to London in 1929 to testify against the proposed union of three East African British territories. His name became known around the world when he was convicted of leading the 1952 Mau Mau independence rebellion and sentenced to seven years in prison. In his 1963 address to the nation, Kenyatta said:

> **We are not to look to the past – racial bitterness, the denial of fundamental rights, the suppression of our culture ... Let there be forgiveness.**

▲ Jomo Kenyatta greeting his followers upon his return from prison.

MAY

28

1588

KING PHILIP II OF SPAIN'S ARMADA SETS SAIL FOR ENGLAND

When his fleet of 130 ships containing nearly 30,000 troops set sail for England, Philip II was king of the world's most powerful empire, ruling much of the New World and Western Europe. England, however, which was under the watchful eye of Protestant Queen Elizabeth I, was out of his grasp. Philip, a Catholic, had been personally affronted when Elizabeth had signed Mary Queen of Scots' death warrant (Mary was a Catholic). To add fuel to the fire, the English navy was helping Dutch rebels to attack Spain's treasure fleet on its journey home from the Caribbean. But this was one battle Philip was not destined to win. When the Armada anchored off the English coast, it was bombarded by English fireships and then decimated at the Battle of Gravelines a couple of months later. Bad weather also had an impact, causing the destruction of many of the ships as they tried to retreat.

MAY

29

1851

TRUTH ADDRESSES THE WOMEN'S RIGHTS CONVENTION IN AKRON

Sojourner Truth was an emancipated slave who had become a preacher; she was also a fierce abolitionist and proponent of civil rights and women's rights. When Truth attended the Ohio Convention, which was organised by the Ohio Women's Rights Movement, she delivered a powerful speech. It became well known, particularly after organiser Frances Dana Gage's retelling was published 12 years later in the *New York Independent*. Truth's exact words are lost, but the passion and fervour of her speech, drawing on her darkest experiences of slavery and misogyny, hold an important place in women's rights history. Marius Robinson, who covered the event for the *Anti-Slavery Bugle*, recalled Truth combatting the arguments of male ministers that women were too weak to take on the responsibility of the vote, with the words, "I have as much muscle as any man and can do as much work as any man. I have ploughed and reaped and husked and chopped and mowed, and can any man do more than that?" But it was Gage's retelling, which repeated the speech's most famous quote, that spoke to the indissoluble connections between sexual, racial and other forms of discrimination before the 15th Amendment gave black men the right to vote.

MAY

30

1431

JOAN OF ARC IS BURNED AT THE STAKE

Joan of Arc was charged with 70 offences, including sorcery, dressing like a man and heresy.

Joan of Arc (Jeanne d'Arc) was a farmer's daughter who would go on to lead the French army into battle during the Hundred Years' War against the English. As a teenager, Joan claimed to have visions and hear the voices of saints; the voices told her to seek an audience with Charles of Valois, whom many believed to be the rightful king of France. She prophesied that Charles would be crowned king – which he was, becoming Charles VII in July 1429. A year later, Joan was captured by Frenchmen loyal to the English King Henry VI and handed over to an ecclesiastical court in English-controlled Rouen, charged with 70 offences, including sorcery, dressing like a man and heresy. She signed a confession promising to change her ways in exchange for a punishment of life imprisonment, but when she refused to change her attire and continued to claim God was speaking directly to her, she signed her own death sentence.

31

2009

AMERICAN PHYSICIAN AND ACTIVIST GEORGE TILLER IS SHOT DEAD

At the time of his death, George Tiller was the medical director of Women's Health Care Services, a clinic in Wichita, Kansas, that provided late-term abortions – it was one of only three in the United States that offered the procedure to women whose foetuses had severe or fatal birth defects or for whom carrying the foetus to term would cause 'substantial and irreversible impairment of a major bodily function'. Tiller was an outspoken abortion rights activist and his clinic was a focus for anti-abortion protesters. Over the years he endured being shot in both arms and his clinic being firebombed. He was ushering and handing out bulletins at his local church when anti-abortion activist Scott Roeder walked up to him and shot him in the eye with a handgun.

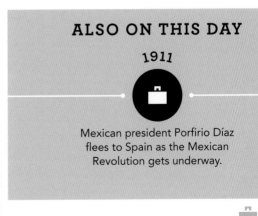

ALSO ON THIS DAY

1911

Mexican president Porfirio Díaz flees to Spain as the Mexican Revolution gets underway.

CHAPTER

6

June

MORMON LEADER BRIGHAM YOUNG IS BORN

Three years after Joseph Smith, the founder of the Church of Jesus Christ of Latter-day Saints, was murdered by an anti-Mormon mob while in custody on charges of treason, missionary Young became the church's second president. Young had been working as a farmer and handyman in upstate New York when he encountered Smith's *Book of Mormon*. He was crucial in keeping the persecuted faith together after Smith's murder, organising an exodus from Illinois via Nebraska to what would become Salt Lake City, Utah. It was there that the Mormon faith flourished, notwithstanding multiple confrontations with the federal government, and the man who had come from humble beginnings left behind a long-lasting legacy, including the university that bears his name.

▲ Brigham Young and his family are shown on their way to church. The image is from 'Scenes in an American Harem' from an 1857 issue of *Harper's Weekly*.

JUNE

2

1863

HARRIET TUBMAN BECOMES THE FIRST BLACK WOMAN TO PLAN AND LEAD A MILITARY RAID

Harriet Tubman was a former slave who had escaped from her owners in Maryland using the 'Underground Railroad' network, only to return to help her family and many others to flee. During the Civil War years, she worked for the Union army – former slaves were able to carry out covert operations in enemy territory because Confederate soldiers tended to underestimate black people's intelligence and did not suspect them of being in cahoots with the Union. The Combahee River raid was one of Tubman's crowning moments. The actions of the African-American soldiers she led helped to liberate 756 slaves and had a devastating impact on the Confederate infrastructure in the region.

After scouting the area and planning the raid, Tubman and Colonel James Montgomery had set off in three US Navy gunboats the night before, accompanied by an all-black infantry regiment and a heavy artillery regiment. In the morning, two of the boats headed upstream, dropping off troops, attacking Confederate soldiers and destroying bridges, stores, cotton fields and houses. As the ships passed, word of the operation spread among the slaves working the fields nearby and, seeing the black faces of the 2nd South Carolina Volunteers, they downed tools and joined them.

▼ Abolitionist leader, Harriet Tubman, far left, was an ex-slave and used the 'Underground Railroad' to escape.

3

1864

THE UNION SUFFERS DEFEAT AT THE BATTLE OF COLD HARBOR

Hailed as the last major victory of the Confederacy in the American Civil War, the Battle of Cold Harbor was one of the Union's most devastating defeats. General Robert E. Lee was one of the US Army's most accomplished soldiers – Lincoln had even offered him command of the federal forces three years earlier – but it was with his Confederate Army of Northern Virginia that Lee made his name. The force proved itself yet again when it engaged Lieutenant General Ulysses S. Grant's Army of the Potomac at the beginning of June near Richmond, Virginia. For the previous month, both sides had dealt heavy blows and suffered loses. At the strategic Old Cold Harbor crossroads, Grant had to wait for reinforcements while Lee's troops dug defensive trenches, giving the Confederacy the upper hand. By the time Grant ordered his troops to attack, it was too late – the Union soldiers struggled to gain any ground, and heavy fire took some 13,000 Union lives. After nine days, Grant was forced to retreat.

4

1913

SUFFRAGETTE EMILY DAVISON STEPS ONTO THE TRACK AT EPSOM

At the Surrey racecourse in England, thousands had turned out for the prestigious Derby horse race, including King George V and Queen Mary. Among the crowd was influential suffragette Emily Wilding Davison. A former teacher, Davison had left her job to devote her time to protesting for women's suffrage. As a member of Emmeline Pankhurst's militant Women's Social and Political Union, she carried out a number of high-profile actions, including hiding in the air ducts of the House of Commons to listen to parliamentary debates. She had faced imprisonment and brutal force-feedings for the cause, but this day would be her last demonstration. As the king's horse, Anmer, rounded the track's final corner, she stepped from behind the protective barrier and held up the suffragette flag. The horse charged into her. She died from her injuries four days later.

JUNE

5

1916

EARL KITCHENER DROWNED

When HMS *Hampshire* was sunk by a German mine in the North Sea, it was carrying Lord Horatio Kitchener and 748 other men; only 12 survived. The British war hero, who had led the British army in Sudan in 1898 and had been appointed Secretary of War at the outbreak of World War I, had recently fallen out of favour after the British defeat against the Turks at Gallipoli. To the public, Kitchener was the face of the 'Your Country Needs You!' recruitment poster, and he embodied the strength of Britain's military strategy. At the time of his death, he had been sent on a diplomatic mission to hold talks with the Tsar of Russia about maintaining a united front against Germany.

▼ British Secretary of War Lord Horatio Herbert Kitchener visits the trenches at Gallipoli, Turkey.

JUNE

6

1968

BOBBY KENNEDY DIES

The night before, New York Senator Robert 'Bobby' Kennedy had won the California presidential primary. It was exciting news for his supporters, who saw John F. Kennedy's younger brother as a second chance, five years after the president's assassination. At the Ambassador Hotel in Los Angeles, Kennedy was making his way to the Embassy Ballroom to deliver his victory speech when he was shot by Sirhan Sirhan in the hotel kitchen. The Palestinian immigrant's main motivation for killing Kennedy seemed to have been the senator's pro-Israeli stance on the Middle East situation. Kennedy's wounds were severe – he had sustained shots to his head, chest and neck – and he died in the early hours of 6th June.

> **We must deal with the causes of the conflict by ensuring a permanent and enforceable guarantee of Israel's right to live secure from invasion.**
>
> ROBERT KENNEDY

▶ Senator Robert Kennedy addresses his constituents and the press at the Ambassador Hotel just prior to his assassination.

66 The vast majority of white people and the vast majority of black people in this country want to live together, want to improve the quality of our life and want justice for all human beings who abide in our land. 99

ROBERT KENNEDY

JUNE

7

2007

BILL GATES DELIVERS ADDRESS AT HARVARD UNIVERSITY

Even though Microsoft founder, Bill Gates had dropped out of Harvard in 1975, he was invited back with open arms 32 years later to deliver the commencement address to that summer's graduates. His opening line was, "Dad, I always told you I'd come back and get my degree." While Gates became famous for launching the world's largest PC software company, it is his philanthropic work, which began after a safari trip to Africa in 1993, that has really set him apart from his contemporaries. Through the Bill and Melinda Gates Foundation he has helped raise billions of dollars for good causes, and has supported a range of social, health and educational programmes around the world.

In his commencement address he said that while he did not regret quitting school early, he did regret what he didn't learn when he was there: "I left Harvard with no real awareness of the awful inequities in the world," he said, "the appalling disparities of health, and wealth, and opportunity that condemn millions of people to lives of despair."

JUNE

8

632

MUSLIM PROPHET MUHAMMAD DIES The founder of Islam was in Medina, in modern-day Saudi Arabia, when he died with his third wife by his side.

JUNE

9

1862

THOMAS JACKSON WINS THE BATTLE OF PORT REPUBLIC This victory marked the end of Confederate General Jackson's successful Shenandoah Valley Campaign.

JUNE

10

1752

FOUNDING FATHER FLIES A KITE IN A THUNDERSTORM Benjamin Franklin was also an avid scientist – using a kite to test lightning's electrical properties.

JUNE

11

1963

NAACP SECRETARY MEDGAR EVERS IS SHOT He campaigned for Mississippi's African-American community for an end to racial segregation and was shot in a racially motivated attack.

JUNE

12

1967

RICHARD AND MILDRED LOVING WIN THEIR CASE The case against the State of Virginia struck down laws banning interracial marriage across the country.

JUNE

13

1547

SULTAN SULEIMAN AGREES TO PEACE WITH FERDINAND I The treaty left Ferdinand, the future Holy Roman Emperor, paying to maintain control of Pannonia (now Hungary).

JUNE

14

1959

PATRIS MIRABAL WITNESSES REVOLUTIONARY MASSACRE Mirabal was a central figure in the fight to bring down the Dominican Republic dictator Rafael Trujillo.

JUNE

15
1215

KING JOHN MEETS WITH HIS BARONS TO SIGN THE MAGNA CARTA

When King John of England wanted to raise finances for a second time to try and retake Normandy, which had been lost to Philip II of France in 1204, his feudal barons pointedly refused. Then they went one step further, assembling an army to capture London, demanding that the king negotiate a power deal with them. His reign under threat, John had no choice but to meet them at Runnymede on the River Thames and sign up to their terms. Drafted by the Archbishop of Canterbury, the Magna Carta consisted of 63 rules that outlined the king's powers and established a council of barons to keep him in check.

▲ 1297 version of the original Magna Carta.

JUNE

16
1487

KING HENRY VII PUTS AN END TO THE WARS OF THE ROSES

John de la Pole, the first Earl of Lincoln, was frustrated with King Henry VII, who had claimed the throne after the House of Lancaster defeated the Yorkists at the Battle of Bosworth Field two years earlier. The Battle of Stoke Field was one final push to unseat Henry in favour of a ten-year-old boy called Lambert Simnel – an impostor who Lincoln believed could be used as a pawn to regain Yorkist control. But the battle further cemented Henry's grip on the throne and officially ended the Wars of the Roses. The rebel troops were poorly armed and severely outnumbered by Henry's forces, and the battle was bloody – almost all the leading Yorkists were killed by the time the fight was over.

The Battle of Stoke Field was one final push to unseat Henry in favour of a ten-year-old boy who Lincoln believed could be used as a pawn to regain Yorkist control.

JUNE

17

1397

MARGARET I OF DENMARK FORMS THE KALMAR UNION

Margaret I was able to rule three kingdoms as regent for almost a quarter of a century.

Margaret was an unlikely ruler – she lived at a time when women were rarely in power, and she was the sixth child of King Valdemar IV of Denmark. But when her father and brother died, it was her son who became the new king. He was too young to rule in his own right, so Margaret reigned as regent, proving herself to be competent and wise. When her husband, King Haakon VI of Norway, passed away shortly before her son, aged just 17, she became regent of Norway too. Then she invaded Sweden with support from the nobles there to seize her third kingdom, leading to the formation of the Kalmar Union, which stayed together, on and off, until 1523. Though eventually succeeded by a rightful male heir – her great-nephew – she was able to rule the three kingdoms as regent for almost a quarter of a century.

JUNE

18

1940

GENERAL CHARLES DE GAULLE MAKES A SPEECH ON BBC RADIO

France had fallen to the Nazi occupiers on 17th June and the French government was preparing to sign an armistice. In England, Prime Minister Winston Churchill had been convincing his War Cabinet that the largely unknown French general, de Gaulle, who would go on to become president, should speak on behalf of the nation on the BBC, rather than France's vice premier, Marshal Pétain, who had declared the armistice. The original broadcast was not recorded but de Gaulle repeated it on 22nd June, saying: "Honour, common sense and the interests of the country require that all free Frenchmen, wherever they be, should continue the fight as best they may … I call upon all Frenchmen who want to remain free to listen to my voice and follow me."

ALSO ON THIS DAY

1815

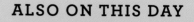

French emperor Napoleon Bonaparte is defeated by allied forces under the Duke of Wellington and Field Marshal Blücher at the Battle of Waterloo in Belgium. This marks the end of the Napoleonic Wars.

JUNE

19

1968

RALPH ABERNATHY LEADS THE POOR PEOPLE'S MARCH

The Poor People's March had been the brainchild of Martin Luther King Jr. He had envisioned a civil rights protest that brought together the nation's poor and cut across all races, to bring about serious anti-poverty legislation. After King's assassination on 4th April, Reverend Ralph Abernathy, the new president of the Southern Christian Leadership Conference and a friend of King's, took the reins. Fifty thousand protesters took to the streets of Washington, DC, demanding a $12 billion economic bill of rights to guarantee employment and end housing discrimination. Organisers and protesters camped out for over a month near the Lincoln Memorial. The area was known as 'Resurrection City'.

> **Martin Luther King Jr had envisioned a civil rights protest that brought together the nation's poor and cut across all races.**

JUNE

20

1789

FRANCE'S NATIONAL ASSEMBLY AGREE TO TENNIS COURT OATH

The Estates General (representatives of the nobility, clergy and common people) had been convened by King Louis XVI of France to help him manage the country's dire financial circumstances. But the members of the Third Estate (those representing the lower clergy and common people) wanted serious change. Coming together with members of the nobility and clergy, they declared themselves a National Assembly, with the aim of forcing Louis to agree to a new constitution, limiting his powers and bringing about social reform for the people of France.

Barred from their regular meeting place at Versailles, the 577 members congregated in Louis' indoor tennis court and swore not to disband until they had achieved their goal. Honoré Mirabeau was the elected representative of the people of Aix-en-Provence, and soon emerged as a *de facto* leader. The barrister and writer was a natural orator. He is reported to have turned to the king's messenger and exclaimed: "Go tell your master that we are here by the will of the people, and that we shall be removed only at the point of a bayonet!"

JUNE

21

1908

FLORA DRUMMOND VISITS ALL SEVEN PROCESSIONS ON WOMEN'S SUNDAY IN LONDON

The militant, headline-grabbing Women's Social and Political Union (WSPU) had decided to try a more peaceful campaigning approach. And after Prime Minister Herbert Asquith challenged the populace to prove it had an appetite for women's suffrage, 500,000 people took to the streets to make their voices heard. It was the largest political demonstration the UK had ever seen. There were seven processions totalling some 30,000 suffragettes, who marched around London and convened in Hyde Park, showing off their infamous purple, green and white colours for the first time. Telegraphist Flora 'the General' Drummond was one of the few working-class leaders of the WSPU. She led some of the country's biggest suffrage demonstrations in England and Scotland, often riding at the front in a military-style uniform. She made her way to each of the processions on Women's Sunday, rallying the crowds.

▼ The arrest of Flora Drummond and Emmeline and Christabel Pankhurst (left to right) at the Women's Social and Political Union offices at Clement's Inn in 1908.

JUNE
22
1944

PRESIDENT FRANKLIN D. ROOSEVELT SIGNS THE GI BILL

Franklin D. Roosevelt came to power at the height of the Great Depression. His 'New Deal' saw the introduction of a number of programmes to help restore the economy and provide support and relief to those who were most severely affected. In the wake of World War II, this was one of the final reforms passed by his administration. The GI Bill aimed to boost the post-war economy by providing the 2.2 million returning servicemen with funding for their lives after leaving the military – for training, mortgages, insurance and counselling, as well as a basic living allowance for those who wanted to return to education. Roosevelt recognised the importance of taking care of those who had sacrificed so much for their country. American veterans continue to benefit from this legislation today.

The GI Bill aimed to boost the post-war economy by providing the 2.2 million returning servicemen with funding for their lives after leaving the military.

JUNE
23
1314

ROBERT THE BRUCE LEADS HIS TROOPS AT BANNOCKBURN

Robert the Bruce's battle-hardened army was 6,000-strong and ready to fight.

In the First War of Scottish Independence, this was a decisive and historic victory for Bruce, who claimed the Scottish throne (Scotland was a province under the English crown at the time). After hearing that the English garrison at Stirling had surrendered to the Scots, King Edward II was forced to take action and mobilised over 12,000 men, the largest body of infantry ever to invade Scotland. But Robert's battle-hardened army was 6,000-strong and ready to fight. They had the geographical advantage, arranging the battleground ready for the English arrival, and the English archers and cavalry proved no match for Scottish spears and brutal guerrilla warfare. On the morning of the second and final day of battle, Robert addressed his men in a rousing speech, invoking the power of the saints, before Mass was said and the fighting could commence.

JUNE

24

1960

THE REPUBLIC OF THE CONGO ELECTS ITS FIRST PM

Patrice Lumumba had launched the Congolese National Movement in 1958 – the first nationwide political party in the Congo, which worked towards independence from Belgium. As civil unrest lead to clashes with the Belgian authorities, a conference in January set the date for independence. After the elections in May, Lumumba emerged as the country's leader and was asked to form a government. Unfortunately, for all Lumumba's idealism, he was now tasked with running a country composed of 200 tribes and a mutinous army. Shortly after independence, Belgian troops returned to try and restore order. Lumumba appealed to the UN for help to oust the Belgians, but was refused. After receiving support from the Soviet Union, Lumumba became a target of America's anti-Communist policies. He was assassinated less than seven months after taking office.

> **Lumumba was now tasked with running a country composed of 200 tribes and a mutinous army.**

JUNE

25

1876

BATTLE OF THE LITTLE BIGHORN

The American government had set deadlines for Native American tribes to move from their homes, where the land was rich with gold, onto designated reservations. When many chose to remain, the federal army moved in to force them off. But General George Armstrong Custer wildly underestimated the number of Sioux, Cheyenne and Arapaho warriors fighting under Sioux chiefs Sitting Bull and Crazy Horse – more than 10,000 at the time of the battle. Against advice, Custer sent 600 of his men into the Little Bighorn Valley where the Native Americans were camped. They were soon overwhelmed by some 3,000 warriors. It took less than an hour for Sitting Bull's and Crazy Horse's men to slaughter all the soldiers. It was the worst US Army defeat in the Plains Indian War.

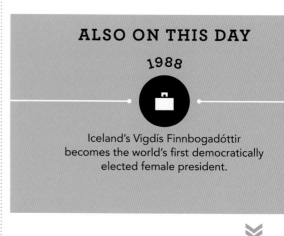

ALSO ON THIS DAY

1988

Iceland's Vigdís Finnbogadóttir becomes the world's first democratically elected female president.

JUNE
26
1948

CLAY OVERSEES THE FIRST DAY OF THE BERLIN AIRLIFTS

At the end of World War II, Germany was divided into occupied zones under Soviet, American, British and French control. Berlin was in the Soviet zone and was itself divided. Russian General Secretary Joseph Stalin attempted to seize total control by depriving the western half of the city of food and supplies. General Lucius Clay, the American-appointed military governor of Germany, controlled an average of 2,500 tons of supplies being flown into West Berlin from England and Western Germany every day. It was a risky logistical challenge that Clay's administration rose to admirably. The blockade lasted until May 1949.

ALSO ON THIS DAY

1963

US President John F. Kennedy declares *Ich bin Berliner* ('I am a citizen of Berlin') following the erection of the Berlin Wall.

JUNE
27
1869

ANARCHIST 'RED EMMA' GOLDMAN IS BORN

Lithuanian-born Emma Goldman became one of the most prominent anarchists of the late 19th and early 20th centuries. She emigrated to the United States and moved to New York in 1889, where she fell in with a radical crowd and was jailed for inciting a riot. She spoke out about workers' rights, free love, birth control and conscription, spending two years in prison opposing the latter. "The history of progress is written in the blood of men and women who have dared to espouse an unpopular cause," she once said, "as, for instance, the black man's right to his body, or the woman's right to her soul." In December 1919, during the first Red Scare, Goldman was declared a subversive alien and sent packing to the Soviet Union.

> **Goldman spoke out about workers' rights, free love, birth control and conscription, spending two years in prison for opposing the latter.**

JUNE

28

1914

ARCHDUKE FRANZ FERDINAND IS ASSASSINATED

Archduke Franz Ferdinand was the heir to the Austro-Hungarian Empire, governing Europe's second-largest country. The streets of Sarajevo, the capital of Bosnia and Herzegovina, were decorated to mark his visit, and people had packed out the wide avenue near the Miljacka River to see the royal couple drive by. After visiting city hall and making a speech, the Archduke's motorcade was on its way to the train station when the car stopped to change direction. A man standing next to the car pulled out a gun and fired twice, hitting Franz Ferdinand in the neck and his wife, Sophie, in the stomach – killing them both.

The attack had been part of a planned assassination involving at least seven young men, who had been stationed along the roadside ready to kill the royal couple. The majority of them were Bosnian Serbs who were resentful towards Austria-Hungary for annexing the Serbian provinces of Bosnia and Herzegovina in 1878 – although it is widely believed that the attack was actually organised by Serbian government officials. The attack gave Austria-Hungary the ammunition it needed to threaten Serbia with war. When the empire's demands were not met, it invaded Serbia on 29th July. And so began the snowball of events that led to World War I.

▼ Franz Ferdinand and his wife, Sophie, leave the Sarajevo Guildhall. They were assassinated five minutes later.

JUNE

29

1974

ISABEL PERÓN IS SWORN IN AS ARGENTINA'S PRESIDENT

Perón was imprisoned for five years, while her country remained under the bloody thumb of military dictatorship.

Her husband, President Juan Perón, was on his deathbed, but that did not stop Isabel Martínez de Perón, Argentina's vice president, from stepping into the role. The former dancer was Perón's third wife (his second was the national treasure, Eva Perón or 'Evita'). When she was sworn in she became the first female head of government in the Western Hemisphere. Her husband had ousted a military dictatorship to gain power this time around, so Mrs Perón's presidency was hanging in the balance before it began. Unfortunately, the country's economic situation got worse after she came to power, and in 1976 she was toppled by another military coup. She was imprisoned for five years, while her country remained under the bloody thumb of military dictatorship.

JUNE

30

1974

ALBERTA WILLIAMS KING IS ASSASSINATED

Alberta Williams King was the mother of the most famous civil rights activist in American history, Dr Martin Luther King Jr, but Williams King was also an active member of the National Association for the Advancement of Colored People and the Women's International League for Peace and Freedom. She raised her son to believe that he could overcome the barriers of segregation, telling him:

❝ You must never feel that you are less than anybody else. You must always feel that you are somebody. ❞

She was playing the organ at Ebenezer Baptist Church one Sunday, where her husband was presiding over morning worship, when Marcus Wayne Chenault Jr, who was on a mission to kill black church ministers, opened fire from the front pew. She was fatally shot – six years after her son had died at the hands of a gunman.

CHAPTER

7

July

JULY

1

1867

JOHN A. MACDONALD BECOMES THE FIRST PM OF THE DOMINION OF CANADA

John A. Macdonald emigrated from Scotland to Kingston, Ontario (in what was then Upper Canada), in 1820, when he was just a boy. As an adult he worked as a barrister – he even defended one of the participants in the Upper Canada Rebellion of 1837. He entered politics at the local level, believing in maintaining strong ties between Canada and Britain. But as he progressed up the ranks to leader of the Liberal–Conservative coalition and Prime Minister of the Province of Canada, he eventually formed a coalition to bring about the Confederation of British North America. The British North America Act created the Dominion of Canada, composed initially of New Brunswick, Nova Scotia, Ontario and Quebec. Under Macdonald's leadership, it expanded to include Prince Edward Island, Manitoba and British Columbia.

▼ A statue of Sir John A. Macdonald stands in Queen's Park in Toronto, Canada.

JULY

2

1908

US SUPREME COURT JUSTICE THURGOOD MARSHALL IS BORN

Marshall's arguments in Brown *vs* Board of Education ended segregation in public schools.

He ended his career in the highest judicial seat in the land, but Marshall had begun it as a lawyer defending African-Americans for the National Association for the Advancement of Colored People. He helped establish the NAACP's Legal Defense Fund – a public-interest law firm that worked on cases that could make change in society, rather than solely for the individual plaintiff. Marshall's victories in front of the Supreme Court (he won 29 cases out of 32), many of them centred on voting and employment rights, criminal justice and discrimination, would form the basis for the 1964 Civil Rights Bill. He is most famously remembered for his arguments in Brown *vs* Board of Education (1954), which ended segregation in public schools. In 1967 President Lyndon Johnson successfully nominated him to the Supreme Court – making him the first African-American on the bench.

JULY

3

1848

SLAVES OF THE DANISH WEST INDIAN ISLANDS ARE EMANCIPATED

Peter Von Scholten was not liked by the other Europeans, mainly plantation owners, living on the Danish West Indian islands of St Thomas, St John and St Croix. In part, probably because he was in charge – he was made governor general in 1827, giving him almost total control over the dominion – but more so because of the changes he introduced. In 1834, former slaves received the same civil rights as Europeans; in 1839, he had schools built for enslaved children; and in 1843, he enforced a rule that meant slaves had Saturdays and Sundays off work. He had been working towards abolition when a slave rebellion started on St Croix in 1848. Under pressure to keep the islands in Danish hands, he abolished slavery on the spot, declaring:

" **Now you are free; you are hereby emancipated.** "

4

1826

FOUNDING FATHERS THOMAS JEFFERSON AND JOHN ADAMS DIE

In July 1776, 13 American colonies had adopted the Declaration of Independence. It had been drafted largely by Thomas Jefferson, and it opened with:

> We hold these truths to be self-evident, that all men are created equal, that they are endowed by their Creator with certain unalienable Rights, that among these are Life, Liberty and the pursuit of Happiness.

It was signed by the 56 men of the Second Continental Congress, including Jefferson and Adams. Both men would go on to be president, but despite their similarities, their political relationship was fraught with rivalry and public criticism. In the last 13 years of their lives, however, they reconciled and wrote frequently to each other. They died five hours apart, on Independence Day.

5

1852

FREDERICK DOUGLASS DELIVERS HIS SPEECH

Frederick Douglass escaped from slavery in 1838, making his way to New York. He became an outspoken critic of slavery and an excellent orator on the subject. He also campaigned for women's suffrage. In 1852 he was invited to deliver a speech at an event commemorating the signing of the Declaration of Independence to an audience of New York abolitionists at Rochester's Corinthian Hall. His words shone a light on the failure of the Declaration to provide equality and justice for all.

"What, to the American slave, is your 4th of July?" Douglas said in the speech's most moving passage.

> I answer: a day that reveals to him, more than all other days in the year, the gross injustice and cruelty to which he is the constant victim.

JULY

6

1535

SIR THOMAS MORE IS EXECUTED

The son of a successful lawyer, Sir Thomas More went into the family business before becoming an undersheriff of London. But it was when he entered King Henry VIII's service in 1517 that he was catapulted into the heart of political matters. He was one of the king's most trusted civil servants and confidants. More wrote speeches, provided advice, and served as the king's chief diplomat. But he was also a Roman Catholic and this would be his downfall. By the time that Henry was trying to obtain a divorce from his first wife, Catherine of Aragon, More had taken the post of Lord Chancellor – the highest-ranking official in the land. More believed that divorce was contrary to Catholic doctrine and declined to sign a letter asking the Pope to permit an annulment. When the king declared himself head of the Anglican Church, More felt forced to resign. He refused to take the Oath of Supremacy, recognising Henry's self-appointed position. As a result, he was arrested and tried for treason, and beheaded shortly after. His last words were:

> **I die the King's good servant, and God's first.**

▼ A depiction of the meeting of Sir Thomas More and his daughter after King Henry VIII had sentenced him to death.

JULY

7

1520

CORTÉS DEFEATS THE MEXICA IN THE BATTLE OF OTUMBA, MEXICO

Hernán Cortés, accompanied by just 600 conquistadors, had set out in 1519 to conquer the Aztec Empire. After being welcomed into the city of Tenochtitlán (present-day Mexico City), he left his lieutenant in charge while he headed to the coast to fight off another conquistador army. While he was gone, his lieutenant led a massacre of the local Mexica (Aztec) people, who understandably turned against their Spanish guests, though Cortés on his return tried to make peace with them.

Forced out of the city, the Spaniards soon found themselves under attack by a large force of Aztec warriors, ordered by the Emperor of the Mexica, Cuitláhuac, who hoped to be rid of them once and for all. When the armies met, it seemed certain that the Spanish would be defeated – they were running low on gunpowder, troops and horsemen – but Cortés made a risky decision to attack the Aztecs' captains. The plan was successful, and without their captains the rest of the Aztec force soon dissipated. Cortés had seen off the Aztecs and secured Spain's future in the region.

JULY

8

1839

AMERICAN PHILANTHROPIST ROCKEFELLER IS BORN During his lifetime John D. Rockefeller created a number of foundations that impacted education, science and medicine.

JULY

9

1793

JOHN GRAVES SIMCOE PASSES THE ACT AGAINST SLAVERY Upper Canada's Lieutenant Governor's act made Upper Canada the first British colony to ban the practice.

JULY

10

138 CE

ROMAN EMPEROR HADRIAN DIES OF HEART FAILURE Hadrian worked to fortify and stabilise the existing territories of the empire. Parts of his wall still stand in Britain.

JULY

11

1789

LOUIS XVI DISMISSES HIS FINANCIAL ADVISOR Jacques Necker's dismissal led to the Storming of the Bastille – a key moment of the French Revolution.

JULY

12

1799

RANJIT SINGH BECOMES MAHARAJA OF THE PUNJAB Ranjit Singh began his 40-year reign of the Punjab at 18 years old. His empire was known for its religious tolerance.

JULY

13

1985

BOB GELDOF ORGANISES LIVE AID CONCERTS The Boomtown Rats singer's concerts and Band Aid's 1984 Christmas single helped raise £30 million for starving people in Africa.

JULY

14

1960

JANE GOODALL ARRIVES AT GOMBE STREAM RESERVE The arrival of the primatologist marked the beginning of her famous study of wild chimpanzees in Tanzania.

JULY

15

1948

AMERICAN GENERAL JOHN PERSHING DIES

By the time he passed away in his sleep at 87 years old, Pershing had spent 62 years on active duty – in 1919 Congress had named him General of the Armies, a special honour meaning that he would continue to be available for military assignments for the rest of his life. Around 300,000 people turned out for his funeral procession, to bid farewell to the man who had led African-American forces in New Mexico against Native American warriors, served in Cuba during the Spanish–American War and commanded the American Expeditionary Forces in World War I. His commanding officer in Cuba, Colonel Theodore Baldwin, once wrote to Pershing saying:

> " I have been in many fights and through the Civil War, but on my word, you were the coolest and bravest man I ever saw under fire in my life. "

JULY

16

1918

NICHOLAS II OF RUSSIA AND HIS FAMILY ARE EXECUTED

Stepping down was probably the most significant act of Nicholas II's reign.

Though his abdication at the end of 1917 had marked the end of the Romanov dynasty's 300-year rule, for the Bolshevik revolutionaries Nicholas still represented old Russia and a regime that they had fought hard to end. Nicholas was not a popular ruler – his sheltered life and his prejudices kept him out of touch with the people. Stepping down was probably the most significant act of his reign. Believing he would be allowed to live out the rest of his life in peace, Nicholas found himself held prisoner in one of his palaces and then in a former governor's residence in Siberia. The Romanovs were seized by the Bolshevik secret police in April 1918. One night, the family of seven were told to dress and go down to the cellar. Eleven executioners then entered the room and fired at the family, killing them all. In 1981 the family were declared saints and martyrs in the Russian Orthodox Church Abroad; 17th July is their feast day.

17
1793

FRENCH REVOLUTIONARY MARAT IS MURDERED

Jean-Paul Marat was a revolutionary leader and Deputy of Paris in the newly formed National Convention. Since 1789 he had published a propagandist journal titled *L'Ami du peuple* (The Friend of the People). Favouring the working classes, it incited mass executions of traitors and contributed to the bloodiest period in the revolution: the Reign of Terror.

His assassin was Charlotte Corday, a moderate republican who believed in a peaceful revolution and constitutional government. When she came to visit, Marat was in the bath – a treatment for the incurable skin disease that left him weak and disfigured. Corday gained access to his bathroom by promising to reveal the names of other moderates, whom Marat would consider revolutionary traitors, but who she actually supported. After reciting the names from a chair beside the bath, she rose up and stabbed Marat in the chest with a knife, killing him instantly.

Marat's revolutionary hero status was cemented on his death with a funeral procession through the streets of Paris and burial at the Panthéon. Corday, who became known as the Angel of Assassination, was tried, convicted and executed within four days of the crime.

18
452

ATTILA THE HUN IS VICTORIOUS AT THE SACK OF AQUILEIA

Attila the Hun ruled at the height of the Hunnic Empire's power, and he did not let his (one and only) defeat at the hands of the Visigoths and the Gauls in the Battle of the Catalaunian Plains a year earlier deter him from invading Italy. His aim was not to conquer the region but to plunder it for its wealth. His war machine first made its way eastward towards the Balkans against the Roman Empire, looting the lands dry as it passed, and then westward to Gaul and Italy. At Aquileia, a centre for finance and government, Attila almost thought of quitting, but instead with renewed vigour he tore through the well-defended city, destroying everything in his path. He careered on throughout the province of Venetia until disease ravaged his men and he was forced to retreat.

ALSO ON THIS DAY

64 AD

The great fire of Rome begins. It burns for six days before it is eventually brought under control. Many believe the Roman emperor, Nero, started the blaze.

JULY

19

1848

THE FIRST WOMEN'S RIGHTS CONVENTION IS ORGANISED

Lucretia Mott had met fellow abolitionist Elizabeth Cady Stanton at the World Anti-Slavery Convention in London eight years earlier, and the two women had set about founding an American national women's rights movement. The convention, which they organised with Martha Wright, Mary Ann McClintock and Jane Hunt, was held at Seneca Falls, New York, and saw 300 people come together to discuss:

the social, civil and religious condition of woman.

On the first day, only women were allowed to take the floor and debate the issues at hand. This led to the creation of the Declaration of Sentiments, a document comprising 12 resolutions that outlined the injustices facing women. It called upon them to stand up for their own 'unalienable rights' mentioned in the American Declaration of Independence.

JULY

20

1923

FRANCISCO 'PANCHO' VILLA IS KILLED

Revolutionary fighter 'Pancho' Villa had joined forces with Emiliano Zapata in 1914 to occupy Mexico City and topple the tyrannical president, Victoriano Huerta. But he became a true legend after crossing the US border in 1916 and attacking the town of Columbus, New Mexico. Angered by American President Woodrow Wilson's support of Huerta's successor, Venustiano Carranza, Villa kidnapped and killed 18 Americans from a Mexican train and then led an army of 1,500 in a raid on Columbus, leaving it burning behind them. Some 4,800 American troops tracked him to Mexico but he evaded capture. Though Villa withdrew from the revolution in 1920 after removing Carranza from power, his enemies did not forget. In what was clearly a planned attack, which some believe was organised by the government, Villa was on his way home from a family christening when gunmen opened fire on the car. Nine bullets killed him instantly.

Villa became a true legend after crossing the US border in 1916 and attacking the town of Columbus, New Mexico.

NEIL ARMSTRONG BECOMES THE FIRST PERSON TO STEP ON THE MOON

Before he joined the National Advisory Committee for Aeronautics, NASA's predecessor, as a research pilot in 1955, Armstrong had already proved himself a hero – as a naval aviator for three years, he flew 78 combat missions in the Korean War – but his role as commander of the Apollo 11 mission in 1969 proved him a leader of the highest calibre.

'This is one small step for (a) man, one giant leap for mankind', were Armstrong's famous words when he became the first person ever to step onto another planetary body, and the first of just 12 so far to have done so. His crew consisted of Buzz Aldrin and Mike Collins; the former joined him on the lunar surface and they spent two hours exploring and setting up experiments. Armstrong never failed to acknowledge that he was part of a much bigger team that had made the landing possible, and to stress the contributions of all the astronauts who came before him.

> 66 **This is one small step for (a) man, one giant leap for mankind.** 99
>
> NEIL ARMSTRONG

▼ This rare shot from fellow moonwalker Buzz Aldrin shows Armstrong at work near the lunar module *Eagle*.

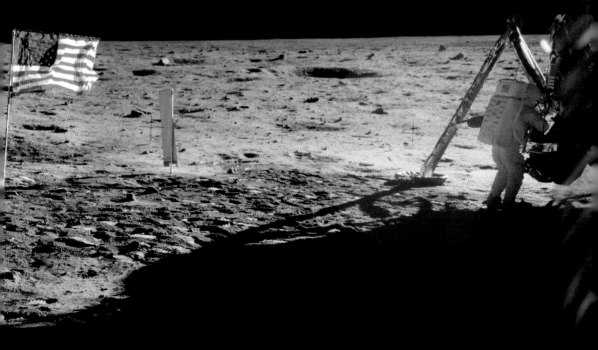

JULY

22

1812

WELLESLEY DEFEATS THE FRENCH IN THE BATTLE OF SALAMANCA

By the time Sir Arthur Wellesley, Duke of Wellington, defeated Napoleon at the Battle of Waterloo in 1815, he had acquired considerable experience in commanding forces, the logistics of battle and the importance of maintaining political influence. He owed much of this to the Peninsular War (1808–14), in which the UK, allied with Portugal and later Spain, fought against the French for control of the Iberian Peninsula. Though noted as a defensive commander, at the Battle of Salamanca he proved himself capable of attacking and manoeuvring on the battlefield – the French lost 14,000 troops, at least double the number of allied losses. The battle was a turning point in the war with the French, whose hold on the peninsula was weakened considerably.

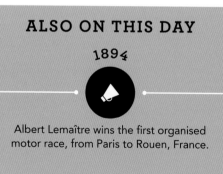

ALSO ON THIS DAY

1894

Albert Lemaître wins the first organised motor race, from Paris to Rouen, France.

JULY

23

1892

ETHIOPIAN EMPEROR HAILE SELASSIE IS BORN

Ethiopia's last emperor, Haile Selassie, was born Ras Tafari. His name started a movement of poor black Jamaicans who believed that Ras Tafari was their messiah and that his coronation in 1930 was the fulfilment of a biblical prophecy. They saw him as God incarnate, come to save them from poverty and deliver them to Africa, the home of their slave ancestors. Though never a Rastafarian himself, Selassie is one of the religion's most important prophets. Nearly 8,000 miles (13,000 km) from Jamaica, in Addis Ababa, Selassie gave Ethiopia a new constitution, restricting parliamentary powers. His country faced war after the invasion of Benito Mussolini's troops in 1935, forcing the emperor into exile. He would later return to power from 1941 until he was overthrown by a military coup in 1975.

Though never a Rastafarian himself, Selassie is one of the religion's most important prophets.

JULY

24

1975

MOZAMBIQUE'S NATIONALISATION PROGRAMME STARTS

Machel's radical stance put an end to forced labour and ethnic discrimination.

At midnight on 24th June, Mozambique became an independent People's Republic, and an independence ceremony was held the next day, where Frelimo's Samora Machel was sworn in as the country's first president. In the month that followed, a constitution was published, relationships were established with other nations and Mozambique took a seat at the Organisation of African Unity. Machel's nationalisation measures included a state takeover of schools, hospitals and private clinics, and the reorganisation of agriculture into communal, state-run farms. Over ten years, Machel's radical stance put an end to forced labour and ethnic discrimination, and boosted investment in education and health care, improving lives for thousands of people. Unfortunately, these improvements were impacted by the insurgency group Mozambique National Resistance, and Machel's presidency ended in 1986 when he died in an airplane crash.

JULY

25

306

CONSTANTINE I IS PROCLAIMED ROMAN EMPEROR

Constantine I had travelled to Britain a year earlier with his father, Emperor Constantius. When Constantius lay dying in 306, he recommended his son as successor to his army, rather than another Caesar (junior emperor). The soldiers at York were happy to oblige and declared Constantine their new leader. He soon got to work uniting the whole Roman Empire, and by 324 he was the sole emperor of a stable and secure Rome, earning himself the title Constantine the Great. His reign saw the establishment of Constantinople (now Istanbul) as the new Roman capital, and he was the first of the civilisation's emperors to allow Christians to worship without persecution – converting to the faith himself and even introducing the celebration of Christmas.

ALSO ON THIS DAY

1554

Queen Mary I of England ('Bloody Mary') marries the future King Philip II of Spain in the hope of providing a male heir to the English throne.

JULY

26

1945

CLEMENT ATTLEE BECOMES BRITISH PM

It was a landslide. Despite running against Winston Churchill's Conservative Party, the Labour Party took 393 seats compared to their opponents' 213 in the 1945 general election. Forty-eight per cent of the public backed Clement Attlee's manifesto pledges (almost all of which he saw enacted), and the former deputy prime minister in Churchill's coalition government held the top job until 1951. In that time, he nationalised one-fifth of the British economy – creating the National Health Service, providing free health care for British citizens throughout their lives, and introducing social security to provide benefits to people when they could no longer work. His other reforms included improving childcare services, establishing laws for land development and improving public access to open land.

ALSO ON THIS DAY

1948

President Harry S. Truman issues an executive order prohibiting racial discrimination in the US military.

JULY

27

1861

MCCLELLAN TAKES COMMAND OF THE ARMY OF THE POTOMAC

He earned himself the nickname 'The Young Napoleon' for his early efforts as a major-general in the American Civil War; he had previously led the Ohio Volunteers, and had seen a lot of action as an engineering officer in the Mexican–American War. George McClellan was ambitious and intelligent. He had spent time travelling in Europe studying the tactics used in the Crimean War (he even designed a horse saddle based on a Russian model he saw there that became standard issue for the American cavalry). That's why the Union General was chosen to take over the troops he would shape to become the famous Army of the Potomac. Although he later lost the post for his reluctance to attack what he perceived to be a more powerful Confederate force, his organisational skills meant that by November of that year he had fortified Washington, DC, and grown the army to 168,000 well-trained men.

> McClellan lost the post for his reluctance to attack what he perceived to be a more powerful Confederate force.

KATE SHEPPARD SUBMITS A PETITION TO NEW ZEALAND'S PARLIAMENT DEMANDING WOMEN'S SUFFRAGE

A few months after Kate Sheppard's petition, on 19th September, the country's governor, Lord Glasgow, signed a new electoral act into law that made New Zealand the first self-governing country where women could vote in parliamentary elections. This had a huge impact on suffrage movements in the neighbouring British colonies of South Australia and Western Australia.

Over 32,000 women had signed the petition – one-tenth of the whole female population – making it impossible for law-makers to ignore public opinion. Sheppard had spearheaded the movement – she was a member of the New Zealand chapter of the Women's Christian Temperance Union, an international suffrage and social reform organisation. Initially, she wanted the right to vote in order to have more influence over the laws related to social issues, particularly prohibition; but she soon recognised the injustice of women being excluded from the political process.

Sheppard wrote widely on the subject of suffrage, and one article that she wrote for a temperance journal struck a chord with women across the country:

> " Is it right that while the loafer, the gambler, the drunkard and even the wife-beater has a vote, earnest, educated and refined women are denied it? "

▲ The National Council of Women of New Zealand gather at their inaugural meeting in Christchurch, 13th April, 1896.

JULY

29

1900

KING UMBERTO I OF ITALY IS ASSASSINATED

◀ Assassination of King Umberto I of Italy by Bresci, in Monza, Italy.

The Italian ruler, King Umerto I, had just attended a sporting competition, where he handed out the prizes, when he retired to his carriage. A few moments later, Italian American Gaetano Bresci fired four shots, hitting the king three times in the chest. He died almost instantly. During his trial for the murder, Bresci explained that he wanted the king dead as revenge for the 1898 Bava-Beccaris massacre, where the army shot at Milanese people protesting food prices outside the Royal Palace. Umberto's 22-year rule was not without controversies like this one, at a time of great social change, but he was also known for expanding the Italian Empire and forging the Triple Alliance with European powers Germany and Austria-Hungary.

> **During his trial Bresci explained that he wanted the king dead as revenge for the 1898 Bava-Beccaris massacre.**

JULY

30

762

CALIPH AL-MANSUR FOUNDS THE CITY OF BAGHDAD

It took four years to construct at great cost and with the sweat and toil of 100,000 people, but Baghdad – or Madinat al-Salam, as the caliph named it, meaning 'city of peace' – soon became one of the most important medieval cities, a centre for trade and scientific achievements. By building a new city, al-Mansur relocated his people away from conflicts in surrounding regions and was able to consolidate his power. The new city was strategically located on an important caravan trade route; the nearby Tigris river meant it also had a good water supply. The ruthless al-Mansur put down a number of revolts in his lifetime and made sure his descendants would ascend to the throne on his death.

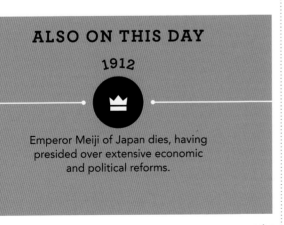

ALSO ON THIS DAY

1912

Emperor Meiji of Japan dies, having presided over extensive economic and political reforms.

JULY

31

1777

LAFAYETTE IS MADE THE CONTINENTAL ARMY'S MAJOR-GENERAL

Despite volunteering his services for free, Lafayette had stiff competition.

After a 54-day transatlantic voyage, avoiding the British frigates sent to detain him, Marquis De Lafayette arrived on South Carolinian shores on 13th June. Nine hundred miles (1,500 km) of overland travel later, he made it to Philadelphia to take up his place as George Washington's second-in-command in the Continental Army. The young and inexperienced Frenchman had heard of the American fight for independence and wanted to play a part in its success, but he was not the only one. And despite volunteering his services for free, he had stiff competition from other foreigners keen to earn a high-ranking position. Lafayette's enthusiasm and passion for the cause won the day, and he soon developed a close bond with Washington and became Major-General at just 19 years of age. Lafayette was a key commander in the battles of Brandywine and Rhode Island and in the siege of Yorktown in 1781.

CHAPTER

8

August

AUGUST

1

1864

GENERAL PHILIP SHERIDAN IS APPOINTED COMMANDER OF THE SHENANDOAH ARMY

The Shenandoah Valley in Virginia was intrinsic to the Confederates' battle plans. Its farms, mills and factories provided the army with the food and supplies it needed, and the railroads served as an important transportation route. In 1864, General Ulysses S. Grant decided to launch a third offensive on the region, and it was General Philip Sheridan whom he tasked with the destruction of the railroads. The powerful general had risen quickly through the ranks, thanks to his influential friends and his actions at Booneville, Stones River and Missionary Ridge. In September, Sheridan's men began 'the Burning', eradicating the Confederates' resources and transforming the landscape into a barren wasteland.

▼ Major General Philip Sheridan and his generals in front of Sheridan's tent, 1864. Sheridan is seated in the middle of the image.

AUGUST
2
1945

'BIG THREE' LEADERS ATTEND THE POTSDAM CONFERENCE FINALE

The last of the World War II negotiation meetings, led by the leaders of the Soviet Union, the United Kingdom and the United States (Joseph Stalin, Winston Churchill – replaced by Clement Attlee during the conference – and Harry Truman), took place over two weeks in Potsdam, Germany. The meeting followed previous discussions at Tehran and Yalta, to help determine the post-war borders in Europe. Outcomes included the joint occupation of Germany, as well as the country's disarmament and demilitarisation; the repeal of Nazi laws and eradication of Nazi influence in education and the judiciary; and the establishment of peace treaties with Germany's allies. There were some disagreements over the economic reparations Germany should pay to the Soviet Union and the fate of Poland's borders, the country having lost territory to the Soviets during the war.

> The meeting followed previous discussions at Tehran and Yalta, to help determine the postwar borders in Europe.

AUGUST
3
1916

IRISH PATRIOT SIR ROGER CASEMENT IS HANGED

Sir Roger Casement committed treason when he sought German backing for an Irish rebellion against the British, which became known as the Easter Rising. He travelled to the United States and to Germany seeking funding and weapons for the cause. The former diplomat had become disillusioned with imperialism while serving in the Congo, where he witnessed the brutal 'Rubber Terror' labour policies under Belgian rule that saw some 15 million people die. His reports on the regime and human rights atrocities in Peru earned him international acclaim and a knighthood. Despite this, and support from renowned writers including Sir Arthur Conan Doyle and W. B. Yeats, he failed to secure a more lenient sentence, and he was hanged at Pentonville Prison, London.

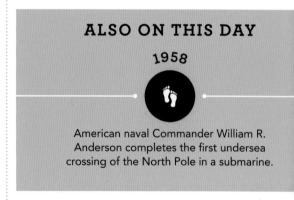

ALSO ON THIS DAY

1958

American naval Commander William R. Anderson completes the first undersea crossing of the North Pole in a submarine.

THE BRITISH ROYAL NAVY PROMOTES JELLICOE TO ADMIRAL

On the very day that Britain declared war on Germany, First Lord of the Admiralty Winston Churchill made the controversial decision to replace Admiral Callaghan with John Jellicoe – giving him command of the grand fleet. The son of a Merchant Navy captain who had joined the force in 1872, Jellicoe had seen action in the Anglo-Egyptian War of 1882 and the Chinese Boxer Rebellion of 1899–1901. The United Kingdom did not need to win the First World War's Battle of Jutland. In fact, it made more strategic sense to keep the British fleet in tact by avoiding a full-scale clash as well as a defeat. Due to Jellicoe's impressive defensive command, Churchill later said he was:

" the only man on either side who could lose the war in an afternoon. "

▼ Jellicoe's tactics were crucial to the Allied forces' victory. He is pictured with his wife below.

FARRAGUT WINS THE BATTLE OF MOBILE BAY

The attack on the heavily fortified Mobile, Alabama, was the landmark naval battle of the American Civil War, and it was won by the Union side. It is most famous for the rallying words of Rear Admiral David Farragut, who was not put off by the Confederate harbour's mine defences, exclaiming,

" Damn the torpedoes, full steam ahead! "

Farragut joined the navy when he was nine years old, and had seen plenty of action in the 54 years since. When his lead ship was demolished by a mine, the rest of the fleet panicked, but Farragut's battle cry and decisive manoeuvring of his own ship saw the rest of the sailors follow him to victory.

ALSO ON THIS DAY

1100

Henry I becomes King of England.

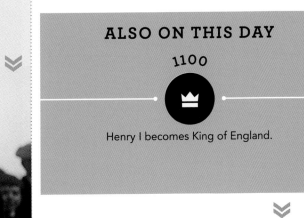

AUGUST
6
1774

SHAKER LEADER MOTHER ANN ARRIVES IN NEW YORK CITY

Ann Lee had joined the 'Shaking Quakers' in her hometown of Manchester, England. The religious sect was known for its vigorous shaking and dancing during worship. But after facing religious persecution and imprisonment for her faith, she had a vision that inspired her to immigrate to America with her husband and some of her followers. They founded a settlement in Albany, New York, and 'Mother Ann', as she became known, and her Shaker movement were soon attracting thousands of new converts. Some Shakers claimed they witnessed her performing miracles, including healing the sick. Forty years after her death in 1784, the religion had settlements across eight states.

ALSO ON THIS DAY

1991

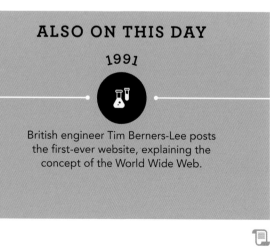

British engineer Tim Berners-Lee posts the first-ever website, explaining the concept of the World Wide Web.

OTTO THE GREAT CROWNS HIMSELF KING OF GERMANY

Otto was fond of titles. He succeeded his father, an elected king, proclaiming himself the new ruler and swiftly crushing the opposition – particularly his brother Henry, who planned to murder him. After years of protecting his domain against invasion from the Magyars of Hungary and the Danes, he invaded Italy, stole the throne from Italian Lord Berengar of Ivrea and called himself King of the Lombards, too. The title of Holy Roman Emperor, first bestowed upon Charlemagne, King of the Franks, in 800, also wound up in Otto's hands in 961 as a reward for helping out Pope John XII by defeating Berengar in battle (the Italian had seized Papal territory). He later had that same pope deposed and replaced with his preferred choice of Leo VIII.

> **Otto invaded Italy, stole the throne from Italian Lord Berengar of Ivrea and called himself King of the Lombards, too.**

◀ This engraving by Francesco Bertolini shows the coronation of Otto the Great and his wife, Adelaide of Burgundy, in St Peter's Basilica in Rome on 2nd February, 962.

ROBERT CAVENDISH, ADVOCATE FOR PEOPLE WITH DISABILITIES, DIES

When he passed away, aged 64, Robert Cavendish was considered a medical phenomenon. When he was diagnosed with polio, he was given three months to live – and that was 36 years before. Cavendish, a former army captain in the King's Royal Rifle Corps, was working in Nairobi, Kenya, founding a tea-broking firm when he contracted the disease. Prior to the development of a vaccine, polio was a debilitating illness that often paralysed its sufferers, and for some made it impossible to breathe without ventilation. This meant that many chronic sufferers, such as Cavendish, were forced to spend the rest of their lives in hospitals.

After a year confined to a hospital bed, Cavendish decided enough was enough and asked his scientist friend Teddy Hall to build him a wheelchair with a portable respirator. It would be the first of a number of inventions tested by Cavendish that would dramatically change the lives of other chronic illness sufferers. He would go on to raise money and petition the government to help build more of these wheelchairs for other people, changing the public perception of disability in the process. He was later awarded an MBE for his work. At the time of his death he was one of the longest-living polio survivors in Great Britain.

AUGUST

9

527

THEODORA IS CROWNED EMPRESS OF THE BYZANTINE EMPIRE

Together with her husband, Justinian I, Theodora would rule for over 21 years during a golden age for the Byzantine Empire. Their marriage was an unusual match – Theodora had worked as an actor, performing acrobatics, dances and stripteases in the Hippodrome, while Justinian was the nephew of the previous emperor. Nevertheless, he saw her as his equal and insisted they be crowned together, rather than Theodora being merely a consort. And the new empress's humble roots did not stop her from being directly involved in affairs of state. When the Nika Revolt broke out in 532, with rioters ransacking the city and proclaiming an army general as the new emperor, it was Theodora who encouraged her husband to hold his ground. According to the contemporary historian Procopius, she declared: "I do not care whether or not it is proper for a woman to give brave counsel to frightened men; but in moments of extreme danger, conscience is the only guide. Every man who is born into the light of day must sooner or later die; and how can an Emperor ever allow himself to become a fugitive?"

AUGUST

10

1581

AKBAR THE GREAT SEIZES KABUL

Akbar the Great's *modus operandi*, in his own words, was: 'A monarch should be ever intent on conquest, otherwise his enemies rise in arms against him.' With this approach, he succeeded in extending the Mogul Empire from Kashmir to the Vindhya Mountains, conquering the whole of northern India. Mirza Muhammad Hakim, ruler of Kabul in present-day Afghanistan, wanted a slice of the pie too, and launched an attack on Mogul-controlled Punjab, wrongly believing he would have the support of other nobles who were against Akbar's religious policies. When he arrived in the Punjab, however, the support failed to materialise and he fled, but not before Akbar's men could take Kabul, the westernmost reach of his domain.

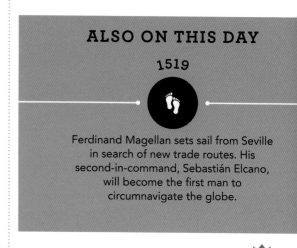

ALSO ON THIS DAY

1519

Ferdinand Magellan sets sail from Seville in search of new trade routes. His second-in-command, Sebastián Elcano, will become the first man to circumnavigate the globe.

AUGUST
11
1919

AMERICAN INDUSTRIALIST ANDREW CARNEGIE DIES

Andrew Carnegie made his fortune from the steel industry, amassing a business worth $480 billion when he sold it in 1901. He then dedicated the next 18 years of his life to philanthropic work. He was a vocal advocate of the redistribution of wealth, believing it was a moral obligation of the rich to improve the lot of the less wealthy. He once said: "The man who dies thus rich, dies disgraced." He also believed strongly that access to education was a key element in personal success. He gave away the bulk of his fortune, including building 2,500 libraries around the world, and funded research into science, world peace and a number of other causes.

ALSO ON THIS DAY

1718

A British fleet under Admiral George Byng destroys Admirals Antonio de Gaztañeta and Fernando Chacón's Spanish fleet off the coast of Sicily during the Battle of Cape Passaro.

AUGUST
12
30 BCE

CLEOPATRA, QUEEN OF EGYPT, COMMITS SUICIDE

By the time she ended her own life, reportedly by using an asp – a poisonous Egyptian snake – Cleopatra had lived a short but very eventful life. She had ruled Egypt, alongside two of her brothers and then her son, since 51 BCE; she had been the lover of Roman emperor Julius Caesar, the most powerful man in the Western world until his assassination; and she had gone on to seduce one of his successors, General Mark Antony. In a *Romeo and Juliet*-style ending, shortly before her death Antony fell on his own sword, believing Cleopatra to be dead. Egypt had been at war with Antony's rival, Octavian (one-third of Rome's Second Triumvirate), and when Octavian arrived in Alexandria, his forces triumphing over hers and Antony's, she killed herself too.

> **Cleopatra had ruled Egypt, alongside two of her brothers and her son. She had also been the lover of Roman emperor Julius Caesar.**

AUGUST

13

1910

REVOLUTIONARY NURSE FLORENCE NIGHTINGALE DIES

Born into a wealthy British family in Italy with all the trappings that went with it – a classical education, a large family estate and a marriage proposal from a man her parents deemed suitable – Florence Nightingale defied others' expectations in order to pursue her passion for nursing. After qualifying as a nurse in Germany, she excelled at a hospital in Middlesex, England, before being tasked with running a nursing staff at the British base hospital in Constantinople (now Istanbul) during the Crimean War of 1853–6. Her team's tireless efforts reduced the British forces'

death rate by two-thirds. Based on her experience, she published a lengthy report proposing significant reforms for military hospitals. She went on to establish St Thomas' Hospital in London and a training school for nurses, and she remained a leading advocate of health-care reform and public sanitation for the rest of her life.

▲ An oil and wood engraving depicting Florence Nightingale at a military hospital during the Crimean War in 1855.

AUGUST
14
1882

ZULU KING CETSHWAYO KAMPANDE MEETS QUEEN VICTORIA

Three years after inflicting a devastating defeat on British military forces at the Battle of Isandlwana, the powerful Zulu king, Cetshwayo kaMpande, was given permission to travel to London to make a case to be reinstated on the throne, hoping to prevent future tribal wars in his home country. The first Zulu to visit London, kaMpande spent a month in the capital, where he met with the queen and Prime Minister William Gladstone. In the years since his army of 40,000, equipped with spears and shields, had claimed the lives of 867 white soldiers on a single day, the ruler had been deposed and imprisoned by the British in South Africa. The visit was successful, but when the British tried to restore kaMpande to the throne a year later, he was forced out by a rival chief.

> **The powerful Zulu king was given permission to travel to London to make a case to be reinstated on the throne.**

AUGUST
15
1057

MACBETH, KING OF SCOTLAND, IS SLAIN

He is known for his role as a murderer in William Shakespeare's eponymous tragedy, but in reality, the 11th-century King Mac Bethad mac Findláich ruled proficiently over Scotland for 17 years. The former Earl of Moray and favoured military commander had come to power after leading a rebellion against King Duncan I. During his reign, he promoted Christianity and imposed law and order across the region. He even led armies across the border into Northumbria, England, to maintain his power. He was killed at the Battle of Lumphanan in Aberdeenshire by Malcolm Canmore, the son of Duncan, whom Macbeth had killed in battle.

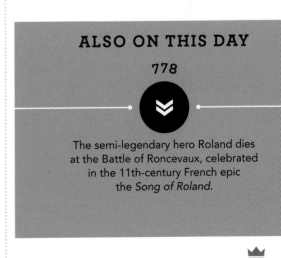

ALSO ON THIS DAY

778

The semi-legendary hero Roland dies at the Battle of Roncevaux, celebrated in the 11th-century French epic the *Song of Roland*.

AUGUST

16

1717

PRINCE EUGENE OF SAVOY OCCUPIES BELGRADE

Prince Eugene of Savoy really wanted to fight for his country, but French King Louis XIV refused him, so he joined up with the Austrians under Emperor Leopold I (he would go on to serve under two more Holy Roman Emperors). There he found success in the Siege of Vienna against the Turks, followed by the Second Turkish War, the Nine Years' War and the War of the Spanish Succession. He was promoted to commander-in-chief of the imperial army in 1697.

> " **Either I will take Belgrade, or the Turks will take me!** "
>
> PRINCE EUGENE

These were his defiant words as he launched a surprise night-time attack on the Turkish (now Serbian) fortress city in 1717. This major trade centre marked the main route for the Turks' invasion into central Europe, so it was of extreme strategic importance. Eugene had raised an army of 100,000 men – the largest he had ever led – and nobles from across Europe came to fight alongside him. When news of his victory got back to Vienna, there was a city-wide celebration.

AUGUST

17

1943

AMERICA WINS THE ALLIED RACE TO MESSINA

The 1943 invasion of Sicily was a World War II operation that involved 450,000 troops and marked the first step in the Allies gaining control of occupied Europe. While 'Operation Husky' had originally seen American General George S. Patton's 7th Army landing on the northwest coast of the island and British Field Marshal Bernard L. Montgomery's 8th Army arriving in the southeast, the Brit ruffled Patton's feathers when he changed the plan, bringing American forces under his own command. Patton wanted to prove his troops equal to the British, so when he was given permission to advance on the city of Agrigento, he took it, powered on to Palermo, and then towards the only escape port left to the enemy: Messina. Patton wrote to Major General Troy Middleton:

> " **This is a horse race in which the prestige of the US Army is at stake. We must take Messina before the British.** "

And he did, arriving several hours ahead of Montgomery, the Americans' reputation intact.

AUGUST
18
1227

GENGHIS KHAN DIES

The Mongol leader, Genghis Khan's name is synonymous with imperial power and fearless mounted warriors, but the man died a quiet death in his sixties when his health and injuries caught up with him. By then he had built one of the largest empires known to man, stretching from China's east coast to the Aral Sea between modern-day Kazakhstan and Uzbekistan. He united the Mongolians by force, promising religious freedom and military protection to those who joined him, and in 1206 was named Genghis Khan, meaning 'Universal Ruler'. On his deathbed, the ruler requested that his passing be kept a secret, so his loyal followers killed anyone who saw his funeral procession on its way back to the Mongol capital. His burial site remains a mystery.

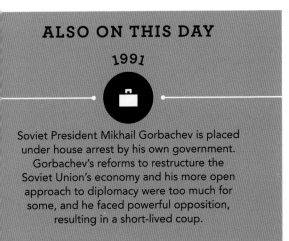

ALSO ON THIS DAY

1991

Soviet President Mikhail Gorbachev is placed under house arrest by his own government. Gorbachev's reforms to restructure the Soviet Union's economy and his more open approach to diplomacy were too much for some, and he faced powerful opposition, resulting in a short-lived coup.

AUGUST
19
1919

PRESIDENT WILSON ARGUES IN FAVOUR OF THE VERSAILLES TREATY

It had taken six long months to agree on the terms of the World War I peace treaty, and now American President Woodrow Wilson had to convince the 96 members of the Senate to agree to it. The House was divided, particularly over Wilson's League of Nations covenant, which promised collective security through an international peace-keeping organisation. A number of senators were vehemently opposed to the treaty, seeing it as a threat to American independence. Though it was unusual for a president to attend such a hearing, Wilson was so certain of the League's benefits and the treaty's importance that he sat before the Senate Foreign Relations Committee to encourage them to accept it. Despite his best efforts, including a tour of the country to drum up public support, the treaty failed to pass, and the United States never joined the League of Nations.

The house was divided, particularly over Wilson's League of Nations covenant.

AUGUST

20

1912

SALVATION ARMY FOUNDER WILLIAM BOOTH DIES

William Booth was not a king or a celebrated prime minister, but his body lay in state for three days in Congress Hall in Clapton, London, while thousands of people filed past to pay their respects. When a memorial service was held a week after his death at London's Olympia exhibition centre, 40,000 people attended.

Together with his wife, Catherine, Booth started a Christian Mission in London's East End in 1865. They called it the Salvation Army, and gave their working-class converts military uniforms and ranks. Their missionaries carried out charity work, feeding the homeless, organising shelters and dealing with the area's entrenched poverty. Twenty-five years later, their 'army' had almost 100,000 dedicated soldiers. Today, the organisation operates in 125 countries.

▼ William Booth, founder of the Salvation Army, 1912.

AUGUST
21
1983

PHILIPPINE SENATOR AQUINO JR IS ASSASSINATED

The founder of the People's Power party and the political opposition to President Ferdinand Marcos, Benigno 'Ninoy' Aquino Jr took a huge risk when he flew to Manila in 1983 from his self-imposed exile in the United States. When he had last been in his home nation, he was a political prisoner of Marcos' martial law regime, after a lengthy trial on fabricated charges of murder and weapons possession. Despite his confinement, he had managed to play a role in the rigged 1978 parliamentary elections, with huge public support. Worried for the fate of his country as Marcos' grip on power loosened, he returned in the vain hope that he could prevent chaos. But it was not to be. Within minutes of stepping off the plane at Manila International Airport, he had been shot dead.

Aquino took a huge risk when he flew to Manila in 1983 from his self-imposed exile in the United States.

AUGUST
22
1485

HENRY TUDOR DEFEATS RICHARD III AT THE BATTLE OF BOSWORTH

The Battle of Bosworth was the last significant battle in the English Wars of the Roses and a key date in British history when 15,000 of Yorkist King Richard III's men took to the marshy field close to the English villages of Dadlington and Stoke Golding in the early hours of the morning. They were up against just 5,000 of Henry Tudor's troops, under the command of Lancastrian general John de Vere, Earl of Oxford. Richard was confident he would win – he even showed up late because he had been celebrating a feast day. But by noon the battle had been won by the inferior force. History's famous imagining of the battle by William Shakespeare was based on the fact that Richard was offered a horse on which to flee:

> **A horse, a horse, my kingdom for a horse.**
>
> RICHARD III IN
> WILLIAM SHAKESPEARE'S *RICHARD III*

Shakespeare had the king say. Richard's remains, discovered in 2012, reveal that he was killed by an axe-like weapon to the back of the head and a sword to the base of his skull.

AUGUST

23

1305

SCOTTISH REBEL WILLIAM WALLACE IS HANGED, DRAWN AND QUARTERED IN LONDON

According to King Edward I, William Wallace had committed high treason and crimes against English civilians, but he was being executed in this bloody and brutal manner because he had weakened the king's control in Scotland and led the Scottish rebels to victory in the Battle of Stirling Bridge eight years previously, among other victories. But by July 1298, heavily outnumbered, the Scots could hold off the English army no longer, and they were defeated at the Battle of Falkirk. Wallace resigned his guardianship of the Scottish army and went into hiding. But the price on his head was high and with many of the Scottish nobles surrendering to the king, he was left vulnerable. Captured in 1305, he was swiftly charged, tried and executed. His head was displayed on a spike on London Bridge, while his limbs were sent to Berwick, Newcastle, Perth and Stirling as a symbol of Edward's dominance over the British Isles.

▲ A painting showing the Scottish rebel, William Wallace, who was brought to trial by King Edward I in 1305.

AUGUST
24
1931

FIRST FEMALE BRITISH CABINET MINISTER LEAVES OFFICE

When Margaret Bondfield was made Minister of Labour in Ramsay Macdonald's 1929 government, she shattered a glass ceiling by becoming the first woman to hold a cabinet post. But as a 'shopgirl' who had risen up the ranks of labour unions, it was her earlier work that set her apart from her peers. Working in London in the 1890s, she took the radical decision to join a union (shopworkers could be sacked for doing so, and there were few women members). She recruited fellow shopgirls and wrote undercover for the Women's Industrial Council, shining a light on the industry. Her campaigns pressured Parliament to take action and improve working conditions with new legislation. She left shopwork behind to serve as assistant secretary to the National Shopworkers' Union and also to campaign with the Women's Co-operative Guild to win a living wage for female shopworkers.

> **When Bondfield was made minister of Labour in 1929, she shattered a glass ceiling.**

AUGUST
25
1944

FRENCH GENERAL JACQUES-PHILIPPE LECLERC ENTERS PARIS

The former infantry captain, Jacques-Philippe Leclerc had refused to accept defeat throughout the years of the German occupation of France. Previously in charge of consolidating Free French Forces in French Equatorial Africa, in 1943 Leclerc was put in charge of forming the French 2nd Armoured Division, which he built in to Free France's most powerful force. He taught them how to use new equipment, execute new tactics and train hard, so they were ready when, the day before D-Day, they joined the Normandy invasion under General George S. Patton. On 25th August, Leclerc led the same army into the French capital, where German resistance had ended that afternoon.

ALSO ON THIS DAY

2009

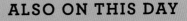

US Senator Edward 'Ted' Kennedy dies from a brain tumour. Youngest brother of John F. Kennedy, Ted served in the Senate for 47 years, making him the third-longest continuously serving senator in American history.

AUGUST
26
1676

BRITAIN'S FIRST 'PM', WALPOLE, IS BORN

Thanks to King George I's distrust of the Tories, Robert Walpole's Whig party was favoured during his reign. In a time before the post of prime minister existed, Walpole was appointed first lord of the treasury, holding this powerful political position for 20 years – an impressive achievement. A puppet master of sorts, he used his royal connections to consolidate the Whigs' power, sought peace with other nations, reduced the national debt and kept taxes low.

In 1735, George II gave him No.10 Downing Street as a gift. Walpole insisted the house be designated for the use of any future first lord of the treasury, setting a precedent that has lasted for centuries.

ALSO ON THIS DAY

1768

Captain James Cook sets sail for Australia and New Zealand in a converted collier, HM Bark *Endeavour*.

AUGUST
27
1983

LORDE SPEAKS AT THE WASHINGTON MARCH FOR JOBS AND FREEDOM

Audre Lorde, the 'Black Lesbian Feminist Poet Mother', was one of the first high-profile black feminists to challenge heteronormative viewpoints. Audre Lorde's appearance at the 20th anniversary of the 1963 March on Washington, DC, when Martin Luther King Jr had given his 'I have a dream' speech (see the opposite page), was not a given. She was there as a representative of the lesbian and gay community, but getting to speak on the steps of the Lincoln Memorial took five months of planning and negotiation. When the march's organisers refused to allow anyone from the National Coalition for Black Lesbians and Gays to speak, other groups threatened to boycott the event. Coretta Scott King stepped in and insisted on Lorde being given a spot. Her speech was just three minutes long, but it was a momentous event for the gay rights movement. Encouraging people to think beyond their preconceived ideas of social injustice she said:

> " There's a war on classism, homophobia, ageism, racism, sexism. We need everyone to fight this war. "

AUGUST

28

1963

MARTIN LUTHER KING JR GIVES HIS 'I HAVE A DREAM' SPEECH

As many as 250,000 people had gathered at the Lincoln Memorial for the March on Washington, DC. It was a one-day protest against racial discrimination that called for Congress to pass the Civil Rights Act. Martin Luther King Jr was the final official speaker of the day and his prepared address was failing to stir the crowds in the way he usually did. That was when singer Mahalia Jackson called out to King to tell the story about 'the dream'. In what became one of the most famous deliveries of all time, and a hugely significant moment in the civil rights movement, King abandoned his prepared speech and obliged: "I say to you today, my friends, even though we face the difficulties of today and tomorrow, I still have a dream. It is a dream deeply rooted in the American dream … I have a dream that my four little children will one day live in a nation where they will not be judged by the colour of their skin but by the content of their character." Carrying the crowd along with him, he ended the speech with some words from a black spiritual:

" **Free at last. Free at last. Thank God Almighty, we are free at last.** "

▼ Martin Luther King Jr delivers his 'I Have a Dream' speech from the steps of the Lincoln Memorial during the March on Washington.

AUGUST
29
1867

ULRICHS SPEAKS OUT PUBLICLY IN DEFENCE OF HOMOSEXUALITY

At the Congress of German Jurists in Munich, civil servant Karl Heinrich Ulrichs was pleading for a resolution that would abolish the sodomy statute in German law. Publishing numerous pamphlets on homosexuality, he was a 19th-century pioneer of the gay rights movement and is believed to be one of the first people to have spoken out publicly on the matter. He described himself as an 'Urning', his term for a gay man, and came to terms with his sexuality, despite the laws and prejudice of the time, saying:

> **I am proud, that I found the courage to deal the initial blow to the hydra of public contempt.**

ALSO ON THIS DAY

1975

Death of Éamon de Valera, Irish politician, third president of the Republic of Ireland.

AUGUST
30
1880

APACHE CHIEF 'DIABLO' ESKINLAW IS KILLED

The Cibecue Creek chief, 'Diablo' Eskinlaw, worked to build good relationships with the whites who were invading his homeland in Arizona. Eleven years before he died, he had travelled to the state's first military outpost, Fort Defiance, and invited three white men to travel to Apache country. This began a period of regular visits between the two peoples. But not all the Apache tribes were so accommodating of the American soldiers. When one warrior killed a white man working at Fort Apache, Diablo killed the culprit to maintain the good relationship he had built. In response, the Americans ordered the tribes to move closer to the fort; they wanted to keep an eye on them, but this led to further fracas between the disparate groups. When the government insisted on the Apaches relocating to a reservation, Diablo turned first on the soldiers and then on the White Mountain Apache who had sided with the Americans. He was killed in a battle near Fort Apache.

Not all tribes were so accommodating of the American soldiers.

AUGUST

31

1997

DIANA, PRINCESS OF WALES, DIES IN A PARIS CAR CRASH

Surgeons tried for two hours to save the life of Diana, Princess of Wales, but to no avail. Her passing, caused by a car crash while Diana was being hounded by paparazzi, led to an outpouring of public grief. One million people lined the streets of London to see her funeral procession, and hundreds of mourners laid flowers at the gates of Kensington Palace, the princess's London home. Diana had been married to Prince Charles and was mother to Princes William and Harry. She was renowned for her charity work, particularly in raising awareness of HIV/AIDS, mental health and landmines. Her work with the International Campaign to Ban Landmines contributed to the signing of the Ottawa Treaty, banning anti-personnel landmines around the world.

▼ Princess Diana is seen walking to promote her campaign against the use of landmines in January 1997, in Angola.

CHAPTER

9

September

SEPTEMBER
1
1864

UNION GENERAL WILLIAM T. SHERMAN CAPTURES ATLANTA AND PREPARES FOR HIS MARCH TO THE SEA

> " I am tired and sick of war. Its glory is all moonshine. "
>
> WILLIAM T. SHERMAN

These were the words of one of the American Civil War's greatest generals, William T. Sherman. Born into an important Ohio family – his father was a Supreme Court justice in Ohio – Sherman, a former soldier who was working at a military academy, returned to the ranks at the outbreak of the Civil War. By the time Ulysses S. Grant had been promoted to Commander of the United States armies,

Sherman had established himself as a capable and fearless leader; he was made commander of all troops in the Western Theater. His personal and controversial brand of 'modern warfare' saw him launch a campaign on Georgia that destroyed everything in its path, civilians included, in an effort to capture the city of Atlanta and help Lincoln's campaign for re-election. With this success under his belt, he stormed onwards to Savannah.

 A contemporary engraving of General Sherman's march to the sea through Georgia, 1864.

SEPTEMBER

2

1945

COMMUNIST LEADER HO CHI MINH DECLARES VIETNAMESE INDEPENDENCE FROM FRANCE

An enormous crowd gathered in Hanoi's Ba Dinh Square to hear Ho Chi Minh declare their country's independence from France, mere hours after Japan had surrendered to the Allied forces. He said:

▲ Ho Chi Minh, founder of the Indochinese Communist Party and President of the Democratic Republic of Vietnam from 1945 is pictured at the border.

> ❝ **All men are born equal. The Creator has given us inviolable rights, life, liberty and happiness.** ❞

Japan had overthrown the Vichy French government earlier in the year and Ho, who had aided the Allies in operations against the Japanese in South China, saw

it as the perfect opportunity to declare his homeland the Democratic Republic of Vietnam. The former cook and seaman had travelled extensively around the world before returning to Vietnam, where he organised exiled Communists into the Viet Minh – a guerrilla organisation working towards independence. It would take 30 more years before his wish for Vietnam was realised.

SEPTEMBER
3
1651

CROMWELL DEFEATS KING CHARLES II AT THE BATTLE OF WORCESTER

After Charles I had been executed in 1649, his son, Charles II, travelled to Scotland to make allies of the Presbyterian Covenanters who supported the king's return to the throne. They had a mutual enemy: the leader of the New Model Army and future Lord Protector of the Commonwealth of England, Oliver Cromwell. While Charles corralled 14,000 Scotsmen to fight his cause as he moved south to England, they were soon overwhelmed by the 28,000 men on Cromwell's side, culminating in the Battle of Worcester. When the Royalists were forced to retreat, many laid down their arms, refusing to fight. Charles narrowly escaped capture, but Cromwell's decisive victory over the Royalist forces marked the end of the English Civil War.

> **While Charles corralled 14,000 Scotsmen to fight his cause as he moved south to England, they were soon overwhelmed by the 28,000 men on Cromwell's side.**

SEPTEMBER
4
467

ODOACER BRINGS DOWN THE WESTERN ROMAN EMPIRE

German chieftain Odoacer became Italy's first king, replacing the long-held title of Western Roman Emperor, and his overthrow of Romulus Augustus on this day is considered to mark the dissolution of the failing empire. He had fought as a mercenary, leading armies for the Romans, before deciding to mutiny and seize power for himself. On 4th September, his troops arrived in the capital, Ravenna, ousting Romulus and declaring Odoacer king. Romulus wasn't popular with the Eastern Roman Empire, which failed to support his leadership, so when Odoacer took over and co-operated with the Senate and Eastern Roman Emperor Zeno, he was able to secure his own position in power for a number of years.

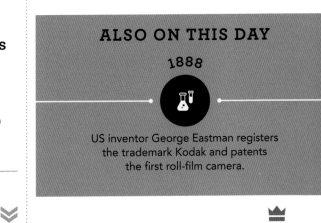

ALSO ON THIS DAY

1888

US inventor George Eastman registers the trademark Kodak and patents the first roll-film camera.

SEPTEMBER

5

1877

OGLALA SIOUX CHIEF CRAZY HORSE IS KILLED

It was a year since Crazy Horse had joined other Sioux leaders to defeat General Custer in the Battle of Little Bighorn. It marked a shocking defeat for the 7th Cavalry, but was one fight among many the Sioux warrior had engaged in to regain the land of his Lakota people and try to maintain their way of life. Needless to say, he was not popular with the US Army, which is how he found himself in custody in 1877. Since the battle, Crazy Horse and his followers had been on the run, but after months of cold and starvation, he decided to hand himself in to the Red Cloud Indian Agency in Nebraska. As he was being brought into a cell at Fort Robinson, there was a scuffle and a soldier speared the chief with a bayonet, killing him.

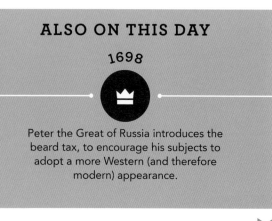

ALSO ON THIS DAY

1698

Peter the Great of Russia introduces the beard tax, to encourage his subjects to adopt a more Western (and therefore modern) appearance.

SEPTEMBER

6

1901

PRESIDENT MCKINLEY IS SHOT AT THE PAN-AMERICAN EXPOSITION

A few years before his tragic death, William McKinley had overseen the US Army victory in the ten-week Spanish–American War of 1898. It had led to the former Union soldier's second presidential election victory in 1900. A year later, he was attending the Pan-American Exposition in Buffalo, New York, where he gave a speech and was shaking hands with the crowd when Leon Czolgosz, a Polish-American anarchist, fired two shots from a .32 calibre revolver. Though the wounds were not too severe, the emergency care on offer was inadequate. The inexperienced surgeon was unable to locate the bullet lodged in the president's stomach and sewed up the wound without removing it. After contracting a serious infection following the surgery, McKinley died eight days later.

> **Though the wounds were not too severe, the emergency care on offer was inadequate.**

SEPTEMBER
7
1191

KING RICHARD I DEFEATS SALADIN AT THE BATTLE OF ARSUF

During the Third Crusade, the English king, Richard 'the Lionheart', meticulously planned the march to recapture the port of Jaffa from the Ayyubid forces led by Saladin. He made sure his 20,000 men were well supplied with water and food, and that they did not march in the midday heat. Crusader armies were known for being undisciplined, but Richard ensured they marched in a tight formation and were not vulnerable to the raids of Ayyubid troops. Having withdrawn his army towards the south, Saladin took a stand near Arsuf, just north of Jaffa, where he planned to break up the Crusaders. But Richard held firm, refusing to let his men break formation to counterattack even when they sustained losses from Saladin's attacks. As they approached Arsuf and the Ayyubid camp, Richard led his knights right into Saladin's army, who had by this point taken heavy losses, forcing them to retreat. The success at Arsuf boosted the Crusaders' morale and proved that Saladin was not invincible.

SEPTEMBER
8
1981

NAACP LEADER ROY WILKINS DIES

Dedicating more than 50 years of his life to advancing civil rights causes, Roy Wilkins held the position of executive director of the National Association for the Advancement of Colored People from 1955 to 1977. Under his leadership, the organisation faced the most testing time in its history – this was the era of bus boycotts and freedom rides, as well as the passing of the Civil Rights Act in 1964 – Wilkins called it a

> " **Magna Carta for the race, a splendid monument for the cause of human rights.** "

– and the Voting Rights Act a year later. Wilkins participated in the March on Washington, the Selma to Montgomery marches, and the 1966 March Against Fear.

SEPTEMBER
9
2015

ELIZABETH II BECOMES BRITAIN'S LONGEST-REIGNING MONARCH

At 63 years and 7 months, Elizabeth II beat the previous record set by her great-great-grandmother, Queen Victoria. On 2nd June, 1953, 8,000 invited guests had looked on as Elizabeth spoke the Coronation Oath and was crowned inside London's Westminster Abbey. Outside, 3 million people waited on the streets. Dr Geoffrey Fisher, the Archbishop of Canterbury, finished off the ceremony by placing St Edward's Crown on the queen's head. The crown dates back to 1661 and is made from solid gold; it had been used to crown her father and grandfather before her. The coronation was a landmark event in broadcasting history, too, with the BBC filming the ceremony from inside the abbey to an estimated audience of 20 million people. In a separate radio broadcast to mark the event, Elizabeth told her subjects:

> " Throughout all my life and with all my heart I shall strive to be worthy of your trust. "

◄ Elizabeth II leaves Westminster Abbey on 2nd June, 1953, at the end of the Coronation Ceremony.

SEPTEMBER
10
1608

JOHN SMITH IS ELECTED COUNCIL PRESIDENT OF JAMESTOWN, VIRGINIA

Jamestown was the first permanent settlement by the English in North America. When the settlers made land in 1607, they were at first governed by a council of the Virginia Company, with John Smith as one of seven councillors; but the adventurer soon set himself apart, leading to his election as council president a year and a half later. The Jamestown settlers had a hard time of it, facing disease, famine and attacks from the local Powhatan people. Smith led expeditions to find food and to map the area. He once faced death at the hands of Chief Wahunsonacock, but was spared (according to Smith's account) thanks to the chief's teenage daughter, known as Pocahontas. Smith's organisational skills and the regulations he enforced saw the settler death toll drop dramatically and the settlement start to take shape.

Smith led expeditions to find food and to map the area.

SEPTEMBER
11
2018

FORMER UN SECRETARY GENERAL KOFI ANNAN LIES IN STATE IN ACCRA

General Kofi Annan, one of Africa's more famous diplomats, died at the age of 80 on 18th August, 2018. For three days, thousands of Ghanaians lined up to file past his coffin. He was the first black African to hold the post of Secretary General of the United Nations, serving in the world's highest diplomatic post from 1997 to 2006, and for his work there he received the Nobel Peace Prize in 2001. Annan learned from a young age that

suffering anywhere concerns people everywhere

and dedicated his career to helping those people, most notably with his work during the HIV/AIDS pandemic and the Iraq War. His first job at the UN was as a World Health Organisation budget officer. When he took over the top job, the UN was on the verge of bankruptcy. He set about restructuring and reforming the institution and established clear goals to reduce disease, hunger and poverty within 15 years of the year 2000.

SEPTEMBER
12
1977

ANTI-APARTHEID ACTIVIST STEVEN BIKO IS KILLED IN PRISON

Born in 1946, Steven Biko went on to become one of the most important South African anti-Apartheid leaders of the 1970s. He was a leading voice in the Black Consciousness Movement; he founded the South African Students' Organisation, an all-black group that sought to overcome oppression by whites; and he helped organise the 1972 Black People's Convention. He was later banned from politics, which prevented him from legally speaking in public, but he persisted, facing arrest and imprisonment multiple times. After one such arrest on his way to a political meeting in August 1977, he faced torturous conditions in prison and beatings that left him with severe head trauma. When he was examined by doctors on 7th September, he was unable to speak or stand. He succumbed to his shocking injuries a few days later. The authorities tried to cover up his death, but international outrage ensued, leading to a UN arms embargo against South Africa a few months later.

SEPTEMBER

13

1993

ISRAELI PREMIER YITZHAK RABIN SHAKES HANDS WITH PLO LEADER YASSER ARAFAT

US President Bill Clinton introduced Israeli Premier Yitzhak Rabin and the Palestine Liberation Organization leader Yasser Arafat to the crowd gathered on the White House lawn, and then the men, former arch-enemies, shook hands. The Declaration of Principles for peace between the Israelis and the Arabs had been signed, with Israel agreeing to withdraw troops from the Gaza Strip and the West Bank within six months. Elections for limited Palestinian self-government in the occupied territories would also be planned. A year later, Rabin signed another historic peace treaty with Jordan's King Hussein, ending 46 years of war. His efforts to promote peace ended in 1995 when he was assassinated by an Israeli extremist.

▼ US President Clinton stands between PLO leader Arafat (right) and Israeli Prime Minister Rabin (left).

SEPTEMBER

14

1975

ELIZABETH ANN SETON IS CANONISED BY THE CATHOLIC CHURCH

In 1809, Elizabeth Ann Seton founded the first Catholic religious order in the United States: the Sisters of Charity of St Joseph in Maryland. She led the order in charity work, establishing orphanages and providing free education to the poorest children. Seton had not been raised Catholic – she only encountered the faith when she travelled to Italy with her husband in 1803 – but she had always been heavily involved with charity work, founding the Society for the Relief of Poor Widows with Small Children in New York a number of years before. She converted to Catholicism after she was widowed and went on to become the first American-born Catholic saint when she was canonised by Pope Paul VI. She died in 1821. Her name now lends itself to the New Jersey Sisters of Charity of Saint Elizabeth.

> **Seton led the order in charity work, establishing orphanages and providing free education to the poorest children.**

SEPTEMBER

15

1940

DOWDING LEADS THE RAF ON A KEY DAY IN THE BATTLE OF BRITAIN

Hugh Dowding had helped to develop Britain's air defence network, which gave the nation an important advantage in the 1940 Battle of Britain. He may have been the oldest RAF senior commander overseeing the decisive air campaign over southern England, but his role at Fighter Command was paramount to victory. On 15th September, just a week after the Germans had changed tactics and started heavily bombing London, they launched a major assault, hoping to finally crush their British opponents. Though the fighting continued for a few weeks after, the Luftwaffe (German Air Force) had underestimated the RAF and on this day suffered their heaviest losses in a month, in large part due to Dowding's command.

▶ Battle of Britain pilots gather on the fifth anniversary of the battle. Air Chief Marshal Lord Dowding, who was commander of RAF Fighter Command during the battle, talks to RAF fighter ace Douglas Bader (second from right).

Hugh Dowding may have been the oldest RAF senior commander overseeing the decisive air campaign over southern England, but his role at Fighter Command was paramount to victory.

SEPTEMBER
16
1810

CATHOLIC PRIEST HIDALGO IGNITES THE MEXICAN REVOLUTION

Later celebrated as Independence Day in Mexico, 16th September was the day Father Miguel Hidalgo, a priest in Dolores, rang the church bells and stood in the pulpit to urge his congregation to rise up against the Spanish Crown. Hidalgo had been recruited to join an underground independence group because he was a respected figure who held great sway with the lower classes – he frequently hosted gatherings at his home where he would discuss whether Spanish rule was just. Within a few minutes of Hidalgo's speech, an army of some 600 men had joined him. And less than two weeks later, 50,000 others joined them to march on Guanajuato to force the Spanish loyalists to surrender. The battle that followed was the beginning of the Mexican War of Independence.

Hidalgo had been recruited to join an underground independence group because he was a respected figure who held great sway with the lower classes.

SEPTEMBER
17
1849

HARRIET TUBMAN MAKES HER ESCAPE

Born on a Maryland plantation, Hariet Tubman's escape from slavery marked the first step in her journey to becoming one of the most influential abolitionists and an icon of American history. She led at least 70 slaves to freedom, although some reports put the figure at closer to 300, using the 'Underground Railroad' network that would be her own salvation. She said,

> **I never ran my train off the track, and I never lost a passenger.**

To make her own escape, she traversed 90 miles (145 km) of the network north to Pennsylvania, where she was able to earn a living as a housekeeper. Fearing for her friends' and family's well-being, she made the brave decision to return to help others flee.

SEPTEMBER

18
1895

BOOKER T. WASHINGTON DELIVERS THE ATLANTA ADDRESS

In what is considered to be one of the most important speeches in American history, African-American educator and leader Booker T. Washington addressed the Cotton States and International Exposition in Atlanta, Georgia – a predominantly white audience – to urge citizens of both races to work together towards social peace. Washington's critics, including W. E. B. Du Bois who referred to the speech as the 'Atlanta Compromise', saw his accommodationist strategy as being in line with the white American's desire to maintain a superior relationship to black Americans. Washington urged white employers to trust blacks and "cast down your bucket where you are", hiring them over European immigrants, and he eased fears about social integration by maintaining that the two races could be "as separate as the fingers, yet one as the hand in all things essential to mutual progress". The speech was extremely well received, and was printed in newspapers across the country, cementing Washington as one of the most influential African-American leaders in America. He went on to advise wealthy industrialists looking to invest in African-American education in the South, and presidents Theodore Roosevelt and William Howard Taft.

SEPTEMBER

19
1846

FUTURE PM OF NEPAL ORDERS MASSACRE Jung Bahadur killed a usurper who had plotted to overthrow the queen during the Kot massacre.

SEPTEMBER

20
451

ROMAN VICTORY HALTS HUN INVASION OF ROMAN GAUL General Flavius Aetius defeats Attila the Hun at the Battle of the Catalaunian Plains (near Châlons-sur-Marne, France).

SEPTEMBER

21
1904

NEZ PERCE LEADER CHIEF JOSEPH DIES Despite trying to avoid conflict with the white invaders, the Native American leader was thought of as a military genius.

SEPTEMBER

22
1828

ZULU KING SHAKA IS ASSASSINATED The South African leader's half-brothers killed him after mental illness saw him slaughter hundreds of his own people.

SEPTEMBER

23
1930

IBN SAUD FORMS THE KINGDOM OF SAUDI ARABIA The merging of Hejaz and Najd ended 30 years of conquests by the king after he had retaken Riyadh in 1902.

SEPTEMBER

24
1827

UNION GENERAL HENRY SLOCUM IS BORN Slocum commanded the XII Corps in the Civil War's Battle of Gettysburg and joined Sherman's March to the Sea.

SEPTEMBER

25
1957

FIRST DAY OF RACIALLY INTEGRATED SCHOOL AT LITTLE ROCK The first black students were escorted by troops from Eisenhower's US Army.

SEPTEMBER
26
1960

KENNEDY VS NIXON IN THE FIRST TELEVISED PRESIDENTIAL DEBATE

John F. Kennedy's closely won victory on 8th November saw him receive 49.7 per cent of the popular vote. His opponent was then-Vice President Richard Nixon. Kennedy was a natural in front of the camera, as the two discussed US domestic policy, while Nixon (who had refused to wear make-up) was less relaxed, although his efforts improved over the subsequent three debates. Even though the next two elections did not feature TV debates, it set a precedent for leadership qualities being pitted against each other on camera, for the public to see, changing the face of American politics forever. It was not the first televised debate in the run-up to an election, however. Adlai Stevenson had challenged Dwight Eisenhower to one four years earlier, and former first lady Eleanor Roosevelt and Maine senator Margaret Chase Smith had debated the issues on TV in their place.

> **It set a precedent for leadership qualities being pitted against each other on camera.**

SEPTEMBER
27
1962

ENVIRONMENTAL CAMPAIGNER CARSON PUBLISHES HER BOOK

Rachel Carson had been a marine biologist and was already a successful author when *Silent Spring* came out. She had spent four years looking into the dangers of DDT, an insecticide popular for killing house flies and mosquitoes. Her research showed the dangerous passage of the chemical through the food chain, and its potential for causing cancer and genetic damage to wildlife, food sources and humans. Carson's book catapulted her to international celebrity. In 1963, when she appeared on a CBS special, 15 million people tuned in to hear what she had to say. And her pioneering work and campaigning paid off: President John F. Kennedy ordered a committee to look into the issues surrounding DDT, and it was soon banned. This in turn led to the creation of the US Environmental Protection Agency.

▷ Environmental campaigner Rachel Carson in coastal Maine.

28

48 BCE

POMPEY THE GREAT IS ASSASSINATED

Pompey, the Roman general and politician who had helped crush the Spartan slave revolt, was in an allegiance with Julius Caesar and Marcus Crassus before Crassus' death in 53 BCE. Then the two remaining generals started competing for power. The senate supported Pompey, who had a superior army, but that did not stop Caesar from outwitting him at the Battle of Pharsalus. Pompey, now a fugitive, fled to Alexandria, Egypt, where he hoped to gain protection from the young King Ptolemy XIII. But the pharaoh was fearful of repercussions for supporting Caesar's rival and when the general disembarked in Egypt, he was stabbed to death.

ALSO ON THIS DAY

1928

Scottish biologist Alexander Fleming accidentally discovers the bactericidal properties of penicillin.

SEPTEMBER
29
1758

LORD HORATIO NELSON IS BORN

Lord Horatio Nelson was a national hero and naval commander who led the British to a series of impressive victories during the Napoleonic Wars. He had previously commanded the *Agamemnon* during the French Revolutionary Wars, losing the sight in his right eye but gaining the respect and admiration of his crew for his bold and decisive leadership.

Nelson was raised in the north Norfolk countryside in the East of England, but the seafaring life saw him leave land behind when he was just 12 years old. In 1801 he was promoted to vice admiral, just four years before the famous Battle of Trafalgar, where he helped to prevent Napoleon's invasion of Britain and where he died at the hands of a French sniper. Hours before, he had sent a message out to the fleet, rallying the troops:

> **England expects that every man will do his duty.**

◀ Nelson's Column in Trafalgar Square, London.

SEPTEMBER
30
1962

LABOUR LEADER CÉSAR CHÁVEZ FOUNDS THE UNITED FARM WORKERS

United Farm Workers came out of the National Farm Workers Association's first convention. The California-based movement ushered in the first farm workers' contracts in the state. César Chávez was the organisation's leader and the man behind the group's non-violent tactics, such as strikes, fasts and a 340-mile (550-km) march from Delano to Sacramento in 1966, to demand a law that would allow farm workers to unionise. He welcomed contributions from people of different ethnicities and backgrounds, and his charismatic and tireless leadership helped make the American people aware of the struggles that workers face in the industry.

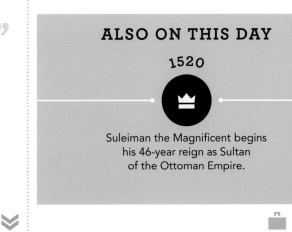

ALSO ON THIS DAY

1520

Suleiman the Magnificent begins his 46-year reign as Sultan of the Ottoman Empire.

CHAPTER

10

October

1

1890

YOSEMITE NATIONAL PARK IS ESTABLISHED THANKS TO ENVIRONMENTAL ACTIVIST JOHN MUIR

John Muir started leading the fight for Yosemite Valley's protection a year before when he found out that the region's meadows were not fully protected by the government – they were being severely damaged by grazing sheep and, at that time, the land was a public trust of California. Together with magazine editor Robert Underwood Johnson, Muir lobbied Congress for the area to receive the status of a national park. The Scottish environmentalist has become known as the 'Father of the National Parks' for his tireless efforts to protect America's wilderness. He also founded the conservation group the Sierra Club.

▲ President Theodore Roosevelt (centre) and John Muir (to the right of the President) at the foot of a redwood tree in California.

OCTOBER

2

1187

SULTAN SALADIN RECAPTURES JERUSALEM FROM THE CRUSADERS

It had been 88 years since the Christian Crusaders had captured the Holy City of Jerusalem during the First Crusade. Born in 1137, Saladin had spent his life at war, fighting first with fellow Muslims to consolidate power, and then against the Crusaders. Jerusalem was protected by a fearsome army, which marched out to meet him, but the Christian forces were plagued with infighting and had poor access to water, so Saladin's soldiers had it easy at the Battle of Hattin, killing almost all the Crusader knights who showed up to fight. With the plains of modern-day Israel and Lebanon undefended, the path to Jerusalem was open. Saladin was able to negotiate a peaceful takeover of the city, and the keys were handed over on 2nd October. He accepted ransoms for the city's residents to go free, and, in contrast to the harsher rule of his Crusader predecessors, Saladin allowed Christians to continue to visit the city without fear of repercussions.

▼ Saladin's arrival in Jerusalem in 1187.

OCTOBER
3
1790

ROSS, PRINCIPAL CHIEF OF THE CHEROKEE NATION, IS BORN

With a Scottish father and a half-Native-American mother, by genetics John Ross was only one-eighth Cherokee, but he was raised in the customs and culture of the Cherokee people. Together with warrior Major Ridge, he led the Cherokee resistance to the white settlers who sought to take their land by bribery, coercion or brute force. They used diplomatic means in Washington, DC, to protect the interests of their people – Ross, who spoke fluent English, was the main negotiator, and served as president of the Cherokee National Council and principal chief of the Cherokee Nation. He helped to draft a constitution for the Cherokee nation, build a government and develop a written language. The Cherokee held out as long as they could against government apathy to settlers' law-breaking and bribery from federal commissioners, before being forced to sign a treaty that saw them relocated after a devastating 800-mile (1,300-km) walk known as the Trail of Tears.

OCTOBER
4
1363

MING LEADER WINS THE BATTLE OF LAKE POYANG

With the Mongol-led Yuan dynasty declining in power, a fight for control of China was being waged between insurgent peasant groups. Zhu Yuanzhang's Ming and Chen Youliang's Han were the front-runners, and they clashed at Lake Poyang at the end of August. The three-day battle, one of the largest in history, was fought on the huge lake near the town of Nanchang. Despite the Han's impressive tower ships, the Ming's smaller, more agile vessels and strong formation won the day. A month-long stand-off ensued, ending with Youliang's death on 4th October – he was struck in the head by an arrow. Yuanzhang went on to become the first emperor of the great Ming dynasty.

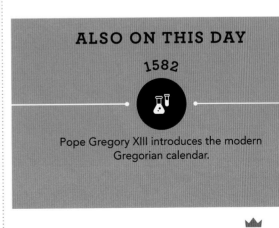

ALSO ON THIS DAY

1582

Pope Gregory XIII introduces the modern Gregorian calendar.

OCTOBER

5

1877

CHIEF JOSEPH SURRENDERS AT BEAR PAW MOUNTAIN

Ending the months-long war which had raged between the US Army and the Nez Perce people, Chief Joseph declared: "Hear me, my chiefs! I am tired. My heart is sick and sad. From where the sun now stands, I will fight no more forever." He wanted his people to be allowed to return to their homeland in the Wallowa Valley, in present-day Oregon, and American General Nelson A. Miles had promised that to them in exchange for their surrender. Despite years of non-violent contact and co-operation, hostilities had been on the rise, culminating in all-out war earlier in the year. Under the skilled leadership of Chief White Bird and Chief Looking Glass, the smaller, more lightly armed Nez Perce forces had successfully thwarted thousands of American soldiers throughout the campaign. The Bear Paw Mountain agreement was not kept by the American government, which sent the survivors to Kansas and Oklahoma, and Chief Joseph lived out the rest of his days on an Indian reservation.

◀ The death of Chief Joseph. Image from *Le Petit Journal*, Paris, October 1904.

OCTOBER

6

1849

HUNGARY'S 13 MARTYRS OF ARAD ARE EXECUTED

The 13 Martyrs of Arad defended their country's right to independence and freedom from the Austrian Empire, but paid for it with their lives. On 15th March the previous year, Hungary's revolution had officially begun. It was one of a number of revolutions across Europe, known as the People's Spring, in which rebels tried to overthrow monarchical and imperial rule. After much fighting, the Hungarians were able to declare independence in April 1849, but Russian intervention soon put an end to any celebration, and the army, led by General Artúr Görgei, was forced to surrender. Though the Russians spared the talented general, the rest of the uprising's military leaders were less fortunate: 13 men were hanged in Arad two days after the revolution ended.

▼ The 13 Martyrs of Arad are executed by the Austrian army under the command of General Haynau.

OCTOBER

7

1929

PM MACDONALD ADDRESSES THE US CONGRESS

Ramsay Macdonald was the first Labour Party prime minister in British history, and the first British prime minister to speak in Congress. The Scotsman had a working-class background and had previously earned his living as a teacher and a journalist. Though a moderate MP, he had a reputation as an intelligent and progressive thinker, shaping the Parliamentary Labour Party from a trade-unionist old man's club into a new party with a clear ideology. With the support of the Liberals, he formed a government in 1924, an important step in the party being taken seriously as a formidable opposition to the Conservatives.
His speech to the US House of Representatives was followed by the finalising of the London Naval Treaty – an important marker in the relationship between these two world powers. The treaty sought to limit military resources and reduce the chance of a second world war. Macdonald said:

" **There can be no war if we do our duty.** "

OCTOBER

8

1480

IVAN THE GREAT TAKES A STAND

Muscovy – a powerful state incorporating the city of Moscow – had been under Mongol rule for over two centuries but Ivan III, Grand Prince of Muscovy, refused to recognise the Great Horde's authority and pay the tribute owed to its ruler, Akhmat Khan. In response, Akhmat and his Polish ally, King Casimir IV, prepared to invade Moscow.

Ivan positioned his army on the bank of the Ugra River, which separated the two realms, knowing that Moscow would be harder to defend if the Horde crossed it. They pushed back Akhmat's army each time they attempted to cross and when Casimir's troops failed to show, Akhmat was forced to retreat, marking the end of the Horde's influence over Russia.

ALSO ON THIS DAY

1829

George Stephenson's *Rocket* locomotive is the only successful competitor at the Rainhill Trials organised by the Liverpool & Manchester Railway.

OCTOBER
9
768

CHARLEMAGNE AND CARLOMAN I BECOME KINGS OF THE FRANKS

Charlemagne would go on to become the first Holy Roman Emperor, but he began life as the son of Pepin the Short, a Frankish ruler whose kingdom, on his death, was divided between Charlemagne and his younger brother Carloman. The two men reigned together for just three years, and then Carloman's sudden death left Charlemagne in charge of the entire kingdom. Determined to expand it, he led a number of military campaigns in Saxony, Lombardy, northern Spain and Bohemia, establishing the Carolingian Empire. He is credited with shaping the structure and customs of much of medieval Europe, particularly through administrative, commercial and legal reforms.

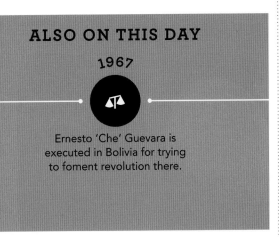

ALSO ON THIS DAY

1967

Ernesto 'Che' Guevara is executed in Bolivia for trying to foment revolution there.

OCTOBER
10
732

CHARLES MARTEL WINS THE BATTLE OF TOURS

Charlemagne's domination of medieval Europe (see left) would not have been possible if it were not for his grandfather, Charles Martel. Martel was the illegitimate son of the mayor of the palace of Austrasia (the territory of which Metz was the capital); this role made him a powerful player in the Frankish kingdom. Because of his claim to power, he was imprisoned for a time. When he escaped, he entered into a power struggle with his father's grandsons, ultimately becoming mayor of the Franks. Securing the Frankish lands, he faced a southern invasion from the Umayyads of Córdoba, led by Emir Abd al-Rahman al-Ghafiqi, and raised the funds to train a professional army for the cause. It paid off: Victory on the battlefield was hard-won, but he cemented his family dynasty and the position of King of the Franks for his son, Pepin.

> Martel faced a southern invasion from the Umayyads of Córdoba... and raised the funds to train a professional army.

OCTOBER

11

1926

BUDDHIST MONK AND PEACE ACTIVIST THICH NHAT HANH IS BORN

Thich Nhat Hạnh was 16 when he entered the Tu Hieu Temple in Hué, Vietnam, in 1942. He went on to found the Engaged Buddhism movement, which worked to renew Vietnamese Buddhism by making it less about contemplation and meditation and more part of the community, particularly during the Vietnam War when many people were suffering. He travelled to the United States to teach and later to campaign for peace in his homeland – he even encouraged Martin Luther King Jr to speak against the war (King later nominated Hạnh for the Nobel Peace Prize). His anti-war stance led to him being exiled from Vietnam for 39 years. He has dedicated his life to Buddhist teaching and wellness, with over 100 books to his name. He was finally allowed to return to Vietnam on supervised visits in 2005.

▼ Thich Nhat Hanh arrives at Hue City, Vietnam, 2007.

OCTOBER

12

322 BCE

ATHENIAN STATESMAN AND ORATOR DEMOSTHENES DIES

Demosthenes is most famous for his *Philippics*, speeches he delivered to rouse Athens against Philip II of Macedonia (he later used the same technique against Philip's son Alexander the Great). His *Third Philippic*, which he gave in 341, was the most effective. "As it is, Philip has conquered your indolence and your indifference," he told his fellow statesmen, as Philip marched into Thrace, threatening the Chersonese and Propontine coasts, "but he has not conquered Athens. You have not been vanquished, you have never even stirred." An impressive alliance against Philip was formed in response. Demosthenes' powers of persuasion resulted in him becoming controller of the navy and being able to implement naval reforms.

OCTOBER

13

54 CE

ROMAN EMPEROR CLAUDIUS IS POISONED

After the assassination of his nephew, Caligula, the 51-year-old Claudius was pronounced emperor. He suffered from a number of disabilities, including a speech impediment, shaky hands and a limp, but he took precautions to avoid suffering the same fate as his predecessor. The Senate underestimated and distrusted him – he carried out trials in private and handed off administrative work to low-class Greeks – but he was smart and ambitious. Even without an impressive military background, he oversaw the conquest of Britain, Lycia, Mauretania and Thrace. Though the circumstances surrounding his death are disputed by historians, it is widely thought that his fourth wife, Agrippina (whose son Nero became Claudius' successor), was behind the poisoning.

ALSO ON THIS DAY

1984

British Prime Minister Margaret Thatcher survives an assassination attempt when a bomb is detonated at the Grand Hotel in Brighton during the Conservative Party Conference.

ALSO ON THIS DAY

1908

Suffragette Margaret Travers Symons becomes the first woman to speak in the House of Commons when she bursts in and shouts 'Votes for Women!'

OCTOBER

14

1066

KING HAROLD II DIES AT THE BATTLE OF HASTINGS

England's last Anglo-Saxon king, Harold II, was killed by men under the command of William the Conqueror, Duke of Normandy. The day-long battle came about after William obtained papal support for an English invasion. He believed he was the rightful heir to Edward the Confessor (the previous king whom Harold had succeeded in January). To make matters worse for Harold, he had just had to fend off another attack by the King of Norway three weeks earlier. He was unprepared for the attack that followed, and when Harold and his nobles were killed, it was all over for the Anglo-Saxons. According to the Bayeux Tapestry, the short-lived king was shot in the eye with an arrow, although some legends suggest he survived the battle and lived out the rest of his years incognito.

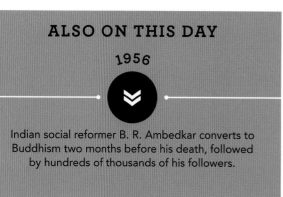

ALSO ON THIS DAY

1956

Indian social reformer B. R. Ambedkar converts to Buddhism two months before his death, followed by hundreds of thousands of his followers.

OCTOBER

15

1987

'AFRICA'S CHE GUEVARA', SANKARA, IS ASSASSINATED

In the 1980s, Thomas Sankara, in his red beret, was an iconic figure for many Africans. He was only 37 years old when he was shot dead by a group of rebel soldiers after being president of Burkina Faso for just four years. Sankara had been a captain in what was then Upper Volta's army, and was a key player in the coup that ended the presidency of Colonel Saye Zerbo in 1982. After a power struggle, he became president in 1983 and adopted radical left-wing policies, such as self-sufficiency, promoting public health and education programmes, tree-planting and banning female genital mutilation. He eschewed fancy cars and first-class flights for economy travel and riding his bicycle. He changed the country's name to Burkina Faso, meaning 'the Land of Upright Men'.

Sankara was only 37 years old when he was shot dead by a group of rebel soldiers after being president of Burkina Faso for just four years.

TOMMIE SMITH AND JOHN CARLOS GIVE THE BLACK POWER SALUTE AT THE SUMMER OLYMPIC GAMES

▲ Tommie Smith (centre) and John Carlos (right), along with Australian silver medalist Peter Norman (left), stand on the podium for victory at the Mexico Olympic Games.

After winning the gold and bronze medals respectively for the 200-metre sprint at the Olympic games in Mexico City, Tommie Smith and John Carlos stood on the podium for the victory ceremony. When the American national anthem played, the two African-Americans raised their black-gloved fists and bowed their heads, a gesture synonymous with the Black Panther Party and the Civil Rights movement. They were shoeless to memorialise black poverty and people who had been lynched. Their actions highlighted the hypocrisy of the treatment of African-Americans, with Smith saying:

> ❝ If I win I am an American, not a black American. But if I did something bad then they would say 'a Negro'. We are black and we are proud of being black. ❞

Their iconic, silent act of protest on the world stage has been emulated many times since. It was condemned at the time for being in breach of the Olympic spirit but it is now seen as a watershed moment.

OCTOBER

17

1912

SUFFRAGETTE EMMELINE PANKHURST SPEAKS AT THE ROYAL ALBERT HALL

> ❝ **I incite this meeting to rebellion!** ❞
>
> EMMELINE PANKHURST

These were Emmeline Pankhurst's words when she addressed the crowds gathered at the prestigious London venue. She had started the Women's Social and Political Union with her daughters in 1903. Tired with the slow progress being made by middle-class suffragists, her organisation targeted working-class women and encouraged more extreme action.

▼ Emmeline Pankhurst speaking at a suffrage rally in Wall Street in 1911.

Its motto was 'deeds not words' and its members became known as 'suffragettes'. Pankhurst had recently been released from a stint in prison for her radical protesting when she told her Albert Hall audience:

> ❝ **Be militant each in your own way.** ❞

Her energy was infectious, and the women responded with more violent actions, leading to harsh prison sentences and shocking treatment by the authorities. Their commitment and suffering helped to win public support for the women's suffrage cause.

OCTOBER

18

1748

THE TREATY OF AIX-LA-CHAPELLE DOUBLES FREDERICK II'S DOMAIN

> " **Princes who wage unjust wars are more cruel than any tyrant ever was.** "
>
> FREDERICK II

Despite his words above, Frederick II of Prussia spent much of his 46-year reign at war. Thanks to the treaty of Aix-la-Chapelle, which was negotiated by Britain and France to end the War of the Austrian Succession, the Prussian king's control over the Austrian province of Silesia was made official (the British and the French were trying to win Frederick's favour before the next war began). As a result of the treaty, his empire grew significantly, both geographically and economically, and he earned himself the name 'Frederick the Great'.

OCTOBER

19

1469

FERDINAND II AND ISABELLA I MARRY

The wedding of the cousins – Ferdinand II and Isabella I – united two of the leading kingdoms of Spain: Aragon and Castile. They promoted the combined nation to world-power status, ushering in one of the most stable administrations in the country's history, and sponsored expeditions to the New World, broadening Spain's empire. But their brutal Inquisition of 1478 would homogenise Spanish society, ridding the country of first Jewish and then Islamic influence. What began as a purely strategic and diplomatic union, resulted in a marriage of trust, love and equality. Ruling as a partnership, their motto was 'The one as much as the other'.

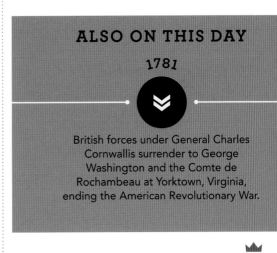

ALSO ON THIS DAY

1781

British forces under General Charles Cornwallis surrender to George Washington and the Comte de Rochambeau at Yorktown, Virginia, ending the American Revolutionary War.

OCTOBER
20
1947

THE HOLLYWOOD TEN STAND UP FOR THEIR CIVIL RIGHTS

The Hollywood ten were some of the darlings of the Golden Age of Hollywood, but that did not protect them against the anti-Communist hearings held by the House Un-American Activities Committee. Most members of elite Hollywood society chose to co-operate, out of a sense of patriotism or for fear of reprisals, but there were ten who refused. They included producers, screenwriters and directors, such as Dalton Trumbo, John Howard Lawson and Herbert Biberman. They claimed their First Amendment rights were being violated, and tried to take the committee to task. They were tried and found guilty for contempt of Congress and were sentenced to a year in prison. Hollywood also blacklisted them, with studio heads refusing to work with them because of their Communist associations.

> **Most members of elite Hollywood society chose to co-operate, out of a sense of patriotism or for fear of reprisals, but there were ten who refused.**

OCTOBER
21
1805

FRANCO-SPANISH FLEET DEFEATED AT THE BATTLE OF TRAFALGAR

British Admiral Horatio Nelson strategically stationed his fleet 40 miles (65 km) off Cádiz in order to decimate Napoleon's fleet, which posed a serious threat to Britain. Under Vice-Admiral Pierre Villeneuve, the Franco-Spanish contingent of 33 ships set sail from Cádiz into the Mediterranean on its way to Naples to support Napoleon's efforts in Austria. But Nelson's 27 ships were waiting.

The British were fewer in number but had a superior naval gunnery and the sailors had been trained for close-range fighting. The battle ended after nearly six hours of gunfire. While the enemy had lost 4,408 souls, British deaths totalled 449. Sadly, that number included Nelson himself.

ALSO ON THIS DAY

1967

In Washington, DC, 100,000 protesters attend the March on the Pentagon, planned by Jerry Rubin and the National Mobilization Committee to End the War in Vietnam.

OCTOBER

22

1957

WEST GERMAN CHANCELLOR KONRAD ADENAUER IS RE-ELECTED

The former mayor of Cologne, Konrad Adenauer had spent part of World War II in prison, accused of being involved in the failed bomb plot to assassinate Adolf Hitler. He had found his way back to power after forming the Christian Democratic Union political party, and then being elected chancellor of the Federal Republic of Germany in 1949. He remained in office until 1963 (when he was 87), steering the German ship through its tumultuous post-war years towards democratic sovereignty. Under his leadership, Germany developed close ties with the United States and France, joining NATO in 1955 and the EEC (European Economic Community) in 1957. He took further steps in diplomacy and reparation: recognising the heinous crimes committed against the Jewish people, he negotiated a compensation agreement with Israel. He also introduced a number of important social policies for the German people, including child allowances, paid maternity leave, unemployment benefits and housing and pension rights.

> **Germany developed close ties with the United States and France, joining NATO in 1955 and the EEC (European Economic Community) in 1957.**

▼ Adenauer meets with foreign ministers as part of his steps in diplomacy and reparation, Paris, 1954.

Canada | France | Germany | Italy | Luxembourg | Netherlands | United Kingdom | United St

OCTOBER
23
1642

PRINCE RUPERT LEADS THE CAVALRY AT EDGEHILL

Prince Rupert of the Rhine led the Royalist cavalry throughout the English Civil War and at the Battle of Edgehill.

OCTOBER
24
1648

EUROPEAN LEADERS SIGN THE TREATY OF WESTPHALIA

After four years of negotiations, 179 representatives signed treaties ending the Thirty Years' War.

OCTOBER
25
1415

HENRY V DEFEATS THE FRENCH AT AGINCOURT

Light armour, powerful longbows and the English king's strong leadership led to victory at the battle.

OCTOBER
26
1979

PRESIDENT PARK CHUNG-HEE IS ASSASSINATED
Despite the controversial regime that led to his death, he is considered one of South Korea's greatest leaders.

OCTOBER
27
1775

GEORGE III SPEAKS ABOUT THE AMERICAN REVOLUTION

Despite the British king raising concerns in Parliament, he lost territories during the American Revolution.

OCTOBER
28
1628

PROTESTANT HUGUENOTS SURRENDER TO LOUIS XIII

The French king's victory at the Siege of La Rochelle after 14 months secured the House of Bourbon's French rule.

OCTOBER
29
539 BCE

CYRUS THE GREAT CONQUERS BABYLONIA
The founder of the Achaemenid Empire was a skilled warrior and diplomat. After his victory he freed the state's Jewish captives.

OCTOBER
30
1503

QUEEN ISABELLA BANS VIOLENCE TOWARDS NATIVE AMERICANS

Queen Isabella of Castile believed that non-Catholics should be forced to convert or be cast out of Spain. Her strong views led to the expulsion of Jews from her homeland. But her forthright ideals did not extend to the Spanish colonies, where she issued decrees protecting the locals, organising the Secretariat of Indian Affairs to make sure they were not persecuted.

It was Isabella who had sponsored Christopher Columbus' first exploratory voyage across the Atlantic to the New World. When he returned with enslaved Native Americans, Isabella was furious. But despite Isabella's decrees and the work of Catholic missionaries who called for Native Americans to be protected by the crown, the practices of slavery, persecution, forced conversions and even genocide persisted. The fate of Native Americans improved somewhat 12 years after Isabella's death, but it was at the expense of another population, when Spain lifted the ban on African slave importation.

OCTOBER
31
1984

INDIAN PM INDIRA GANDHI IS SHOT DEAD BY TWO OF HER OWN BODYGUARDS

Indira Gandhi, the country's first female prime minister, became a hate figure for some of the Indian population after ordering the Indian army to occupy a Sikh temple. Operation Blue Star saw hundreds of people lose their lives when the military stormed the Harmandir Sahib temple complex in Amritsar, Punjab, in June 1984. It had become a stronghold for a group of militant Sikhs who were protesting in favour of a Sikh homeland. While leaving her home a few months later, on her way to a TV recording, two Sikh men, Beant Singh and Satwant Singh, shot at her a dozen times. Her assassination led to vicious mob attacks on the country's Sikh community.

▲ Gandhi speaks in Jaipur, six days before she was assassinated.

CHAPTER

11

November

NOVEMBER
1
1922

ATATÜRK PUTS AN END TO THE OTTOMAN EMPIRE

When surnames were introduced in Turkey in 1935, the people gave Mustafa Kemal his: Atatürk, meaning 'Father of the Turks'. Thirteen years earlier, he had proclaimed the Republic of Turkey after launching a nationalist revolution in 1919. The experienced military commander and his supporters were opposed to the World War I peace settlement that saw Turkey's borders redrawn, omitting areas of Anatolia, the Turkish people's traditional homeland. The republican government swiftly abolished the Sultanate of Constantinople and expelled the last sultan, Mehmed VI, and in a matter of months a new treaty emerged that established the sovereignty of the Republic of Turkey. Atatürk's single-party rule lasted until 1945, in which time he implemented vast social and political reforms, including the introduction of Western legal codes and the Western alphabet, and the emancipation of women.

▼ Mustafa Kemal (Atatürk) in Bursa, Turkey.

NOVEMBER

2

1917

ZIONIST LIONEL WALTER ROTHSCHILD IS PRESENTED WITH THE BALFOUR DECLARATION

The Balfour Declaration remains one of the most significant and controversial documents relating to the Israeli–Palestinian conflict – a public letter written to a leading figure of the British Jewish community, stating Britain's support for a Jewish 'national home' in Palestine. The letter's author was British Foreign Secretary Arthur Balfour, who believed that showing backing for Zionists would help shore up Russian and American involvement in World War I, as well as bringing in much-needed funding from British Zionists. The recipient was Lionel Walter Rothschild, a former Conservative MP from one of Britain's wealthiest Jewish families and an avid zoologist. After the war, Rothschild continued to support the Zionist movement, reaching out for Arab support from Emir Faisal of Arabia.

▼ Lionel Walter Rothschild with his famed zebra carriage, which he frequently drove through London.

OLYMPE DE GOUGES IS GUILLOTINED

Born Marie Gouze, Olympe De Gouges changed her name when she arrived in Paris as a widow in her twenties. She was a prominent playwright, supporter of the Girondin faction and pamphleteer, proposing substantial reforms to the new revolutionary government. Her most famous publication was the *Declaration of the Rights of Woman and Citizen*, which chastised the government for applauding a revolution that endowed men with the freedoms they wanted while ignoring the rights of women. She wrote:

> " **Women, when will you stop being blind? What advantages did the Revolution bring you?** "

After the fall of the Girondins, the staunch feminist was arrested and condemned to death for her views.

BAPTIST MINISTER JACKSON LAUNCHES HIS PRESIDENCY CAMPAIGN

Jesse Jackson's civil rights activism began in Greenville County, South Carolina, when he was 19. Together with seven others, he entered a 'whites only' library, and was arrested and jailed. Throughout the 1960s he was involved in a number of important civil rights actions, including the Selma Marches in Alabama in 1965. He headed Operation Breadbasket – the economic arm of the Southern Christian Leadership Conference – organising mass boycotts by black consumers in order to pressure white business owners to hire black employees or to spend their money at firms owned by black people. Jackson campaigned for the democratic presidential nomination for the 1984 and 1988 elections, although he was unlucky both times.

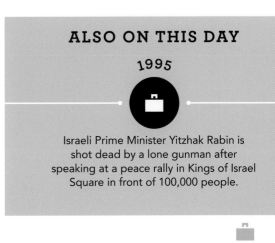

ALSO ON THIS DAY

1995

Israeli Prime Minister Yitzhak Rabin is shot dead by a lone gunman after speaking at a peace rally in Kings of Israel Square in front of 100,000 people.

NOVEMBER

5

1985

NYERERE, PRESIDENT OF TANZANIA, LEAVES OFFICE

Julius Nyerere, one of the first post-colonial African leaders to voluntarily step down from power, was revered by many of his people – his nickname in much of Africa is Mwalimu, meaning 'teacher'. Independence came to Tanganyika (later Tanzania) in large part thanks to the relationship he had built with the British. Despite his country being plagued by economic troubles, corruption and Idi Amin's Ugandan invasion, under his leadership there were advances in health, mass literacy programmes and agricultural collectivisation – he hoped that the country could become economically self-sufficient. He also fought for the rights of other nations, including South Africa, South West Africa (now Namibia) and Rhodesia (now Zimbabwe).

ALSO ON THIS DAY

1757

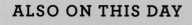

Seven Years' War: Frederick the Great of Prussia defeats the allied armies of France and the Holy Roman Empire at the Battle of Rossbach, Saxony.

NOVEMBER

6

1913

INDIAN ACTIVIST GANDHI IS ARRESTED IN SOUTH AFRICA

Mohandas Gandhi had moved to South Africa from his native India in 1893. He was a young, unknown barrister hired as a lawyer for an Indian businessman. After facing discrimination there, he developed his non-violent approach to protest. He led Indian expatriates in protests against a law that required Indians to register with the 'Asiatic Department' and carry registration cards, and against a discriminatory tax on Indians. He spent 21 years in South Africa and was jailed four times. His last arrest, on 6th November, 1913, came when he led a march of more than 2,000 people. He left South Africa a year later, and used all he had learned, and the resilience he had built up, to campaign for India's independence from Britain. He was assassinated in 1948, one year after seeing his hard work come to fruition.

Mohandas Gandhi spent 21 years in South Africa and was jailed four times.

NOVEMBER

7

1879

RUSSIAN REVOLUTIONARY
LEON TROTSKY IS BORN

Leon Trotsky was one of 20th-century Russia's most significant figures but started life in Ukraine, the son of hardworking Jewish farmers. The family was successful, meaning there was money to pay for Trotsky's education in Odessa. In this port city, rich with trade and culture, and with great disparity of wealth, he developed a gift for languages and learned about the Revolutionary Movement. This led him to the shipbuilding city of Nikolayev (Mykolaiv), where he started a trade union and expounded socialist doctrine to the factory workers. He was imprisoned without trial for inciting revolution and used his four-year jail term in Siberia to study and further his understanding of Marxism. When he made his escape in 1902, he travelled to London and worked for the Russian émigré newspaper *Iskra* (*The Spark*). There he met other socialist writers, one of whom was Vladimir Lenin.

▼ Lenin, Trotsky and Kamenev (centre) in Moscow, Russia, 1920.

NOVEMBER
8
1904

THEODORE ROOSEVELT IS ELECTED PRESIDENT OF THE US

Theodore Roosevelt was already in the White House, but this was the first time the people had chosen to put him in the Oval Office. The former vice president had inherited the job when he was only 42, after President William McKinley's assassination (the Republican pair had campaigned together in 1901, winning a landslide victory). His youth and enthusiasm were infectious – he saw government as the mediator on behalf of the people between the powerful forces of a capitalist society, bringing suits against industry giants who were trying to control trade and protecting huge swathes of American wilderness from development. When the people went to the polls in 1904, they chose to keep him.

▼ Theodore Roosevelt during a tour in support of military preparedness.

NOVEMBER

9

1799

NAPOLEON BONAPARTE LEADS THE *COUP DE BRUMAIRE*

By the end of the 18th century, the French king was dead and the population had lived through the Great Terror, in which thousands of people had been guillotined, both moderate republicans and then, later, radical Jacobins. The country was being run by a regime known as the Directorate, when Corsican general Napoleon Bonaparte returned to France after many successful military campaigns abroad. The famous soldier was seen as a potential saviour of France, and on this day he marched into the Council of the Ancients (the upper chamber of government) and demanded regime change. With an army of thousands backing him, this intimidation worked, and the constitution was changed to reflect the country's new leadership – a system of absolute power belonging to one man, Napoleon, known as First Consul.

> **Napoleon was seen as a potential saviour of France.**

NOVEMBER

10

1775

THE US MARINES ARE FORMED – NICHOLAS LEADS THE CHARGE

When the American Revolution broke out in April 1775, Sam Nicholas was still running a tavern business in Philadelphia, through which he had become well connected. It was this that led the Second Continental Congress to him when they wanted help recruiting a marine corps to serve with the Continental Navy as landing forces and to provide security aboard ship for the fleet. As a result, Nicholas was appointed captain of marines and five days later the Continental Marines (later named the US Marine Corps) was born.

Recruitment began in earnest, with Nicholas managing to raise five companies of eager marines by year's end. Despite having little military experience, Nicholas took charge of one of the marine detachments aboard the frigate *Alfred*, leading a landing at Nassau and capturing two British ships the following year. After the enemy had evacuated Philadelphia, he returned home and established the marine barracks, and served, effectively, as the first commandant of the Marine Corps.

NOVEMBER 11 1775

MOHAWK CHIEF BRANT PETITIONS THE CROWN
Joseph Brant and Guy Johnson (British Superintendent for Northern Indian Affairs) petition the crown.

NOVEMBER 12 1035

CNUT THE GREAT DIES
Cnut (ruler of Denmark and Norway) fought Anglo-Saxon King Edmund Ironside to gain control of England. He later died in Shaftesbury.

NOVEMBER 13 354

THEOLOGIAN AUGUSTINE OF HIPPO IS BORN The Roman African future saint was born in Thagaste in present-day Algeria. He is a key figure in Western Christianity.

NOVEMBER 14 1983

LECH WAŁĘSA IS RELEASED
After 11 months in custody the leader of Poland's National Federation of Unions was released from prison.

NOVEMBER 15 1919

NANCY ASTOR IS ELECTED TO THE BRITISH PARLIAMENT
Astor was the Conservative MP for Plymouth Sutton until 1945 and was the first woman to take her seat in Parliament.

NOVEMBER 16 1532

THE LAST INCA EMPEROR IS CAPTURED BY PIZARRO
The Spanish trial and execution of Emperor Atahualpa in August 1933 ended the 300-year-old Inca civilisation.

NOVEMBER 17 1942

NEW COMMANDER-IN-CHIEF OF WESTERN APPROACHES
Admiral Max Horton improved anti-U-boat operations and convoy protection during the Battle of the Atlantic.

NOVEMBER 18 1812

KUTUZOV DEFEATS NAPOLEON'S GRANDE ARMÉE AT KRASNOI

Russian General Mikhail Illarionovich Kutuzov was one of 19th-century Russia's finest commanders. And it was his public popularity that had persuaded Tsar Alexander to appoint him commander in chief of the Russian forces, and a prince to boot, in August 1812. The Napoleonic Wars had arrived in Russia in June 1812, but the French emperor had yet to win a decisive victory; the Russians kept retreating, forcing him to press on despite an unsustainable supply chain and the encroaching winter. After waiting for a surrender that never came, Napoleon tried to retreat, but Kutuzov had other ideas, engaging the French army in a series of minor engagements that wore them down and forced them to face the harsh Russian winter. Preserving his own forces from facing another major battle, Kutuzov demonstrated his strategic prowess and the loyalty and devotion he felt towards his troops.

> ### Napoleon tried to retreat, but Kutuzov had other ideas.

NOVEMBER
19
1863

PRESIDENT ABRAHAM LINCOLN DELIVERS HIS GETTYSBURG ADDRESS

In a meagre 242 words, Abraham Lincoln addressed the people gathered at the 17-acre (7-hectare) cemetery at Gettysburg, Pennsylvania, which was being dedicated as a resting place for the 7,500 fallen soldiers of the great Civil War battle there, four months earlier. After a two-hour address from popular orator Edward Everett, Lincoln began: "Four score and seven years ago, our fathers brought forth on this continent, a new nation, conceived in liberty, and dedicated to the proposition that all men are created equal." He went on to express the importance of pushing on with the war, so that the buried soldiers would not have died in vain, and that democracy in its purest form, "government of the people, by the people, for the people, shall not perish from the earth."

▼ A painting depicting Abraham Lincoln making the Gettysburg Address at the dedication of the Soldiers' National Cemetery in Gettysburg, Pennsylvania.

NOVEMBER
20
1755

WILLIAM PITT THE ELDER RESIGNS

With tensions between France and Britain in the American colonies at breaking point, Whig minister Pitt was concerned that a European-wide conflict could follow. He was forced to resign for voicing his views in the House of Commons. Known as the 'Great Commoner' for his parliamentary skill and his role in forging the British Empire, Pitt was a popular politician who wielded great influence in 18th-century Britain. Down but not out, he soon formed alliances with Lord Newcastle and the Duke of Devonshire, which gave him control over the Seven Years' War. He said,

> **I am sure I can save this country, and nobody else can.**

He sent expeditions to America to secure Canada's conquest, to India to protect the trade interests of the British East India Company, and to Prussia to keep the French occupied on the continent. His determination became too much for France, and the Treaty of Paris ensured Britain's imperial dominance around the world.

NOVEMBER
21
1620

THE PILGRIM FATHERS SIGN THE *MAYFLOWER* COMPACT

William Bradford was one of the 102 colonists who later became known as the Pilgrim Fathers, who settled in Plymouth (in present-day Massachusetts) – New England's first permanent colony. Some of the *Mayflower*'s passengers, including Bradford, were members of the English Separatist Church, a radical Puritan faction, and had travelled there in the hope of religious freedom. All the male settlers signed the New World's first social contract, agreeing to be part of a 'civil body politic'. It contained the community's founding principles. Between 1622 and 1656, Bradford was elected governor 30 times. As acting judge and treasurer he was a powerful influence on the colony, including drafting its legal code.

All the male settlers signed the New World's first social contract, agreeing to be part of a 'civil body politic'.

ANGELA MERKEL BECOMES THE FIRST FEMALE CHANCELLOR OF GERMANY

Angela Merkel had joined the centre-right Christian Democrats in 1990, two months before Germany's reunification. The former chemist was given the position of Minister for Women and Youth in Chancellor Helmut Kohl's government. Ten years later, in the wake of Kohl's resignation after a scandal, she was elected the party's leader. In the years that followed her first election win, she had to handle the potentially catastrophic impacts of the European financial crisis. In 2015 she was named *Time Magazine*'s Person of the Year for her handling of the refugee emergency, opening Germany's borders to asylum seekers. She resigns in 2021, after four election wins and what will be 16 years in the job.

▶ Angela Merkel holds a press conference after the 2017 general election in Berlin, Germany.

NOVEMBER

23

1803

AMERICAN ABOLITIONIST WELD IS BORN

Theodore Dwight Weld was a founding member of the American Anti-Slavery Society, set up in 1833, and the leader of a group of men and women, known as the Seventy, who regularly left their hometowns and states to travel to places where they, and their abolitionist views, were not welcome. Through pamphlets, orations and debate they opened people's eyes to the horrors of the slave trade and recruited new abolitionists to their cause. Among Weld's personal converts was Harriet Beecher Stowe. In fact, one of Weld's pamphlets is said to have inspired Stowe's hugely influential anti-slavery novel *Uncle Tom's Cabin*.

ALSO ON THIS DAY

1174

Saladin, already Sultan of Egypt, seizes control of Damascus, Syria.

NOVEMBER

24

1993

THE US SENATE PASSES THE BRADY BILL BY UNANIMOUS CONSENT

In 1991, former President Ronald Reagan announced his support for the Brady Bill. It had been ten years since the assassination attempt on the president's life, in which White House press secretary Jim Brady was also shot, leaving him paralysed for life. Jim, together with his wife Sarah, founded the Brady Campaign to help prevent further gun violence through changing the law. Their efforts resulted in the passing of the Brady Handgun Violence Prevention Act, which was signed by President Bill Clinton just six days after the unanimous Senate decision, and required that every sale of a gun by a licensed dealer be referred to law enforcement for a background check. Although the act has blocked more than three million prohibited gun purchases since its passing, the number of fatal civilian shootings in the US has continued to rise.

> Jim, together with his wife Sarah, founded the Brady Campaign to help prevent further gun violence through changing the law.

FORMER UN SECRETARY GENERAL U THANT DIES

U Thant passed away from lung cancer just three years after he had left his record ten-year, one-month stint as the third UN secretary general. He took over the role at short notice when Dag Hammarskjöld was killed in an air crash. The Burmese diplomat was the first non-European to be appointed, and steered the organisation through the 1960s, strengthening its position and importance in global affairs. He was integral in defusing the Cuban missile crisis, advocated against apartheid in South Africa, promoted environmentalism with the First Earth Summit, ended the civil war in the Congo and actively worked towards a peaceful outcome in Vietnam.

▲ U Thant (left), Burmese secretary general of the United Nations, is pictured with Congo's president Joseph Mobutu (right), during the meeting of African leaders in Kinshasa, Democratic Republic of Congo.

ALSO ON THIS DAY

1120

William Adelin, heir to the English throne, is among those drowned when the *White Ship* sinks in the English Channel, resulting in a succession dispute and the civil war known as the Anarchy.

NOVEMBER

26

43 BCE

ROME'S SECOND TRIUMVIRATE IS FORMED

After Julius Caesar's assassination, his killers fled Rome, leaving his loyal deputies, Marcus Aemilius Lepidus and Mark Antony, in charge. Antony insisted on a public reading of the ruler's will, in which it was revealed that Caesar had left most of his estate to his great-nephew and adopted son and heir Gaius Octavian (who would later be known as Augustus). The assassins' hopes of reinstating a functioning republic were initially crushed when they and Octavian entered a power struggle for ultimate control of the Roman Empire. But they reconciled, forming the Second Triumvirate: an official, legal alliance between the three of them that lasted for ten years. After Lepidus' death, Octavian and Antony would return to their warring ways, with the former coming out on top. He became the first emperor of the Roman Empire, ruling for 41 years.

Antony insisted on a public reading of the ruler's will.

NOVEMBER

27

1978

HARVEY MILK IS ASSASSINATED

Known as the Mayor of Castro Street, Supervisor Harvey Milk was one of the United States' first openly gay politicians. He co-founded the Castro Village Association – a group to unite the area's gay business owners – and the San Francisco Gay Democratic Club, to build up political support for his campaign to be elected to the city's Board of Supervisors. After unsuccessful runs in 1973 and 1975, he broadened his appeal beyond the gay community, his policies focusing on low-income housing and day-care provisions for working mothers. In 1977 he was elected, and spearheaded a bill to ban sexual orientation discrimination in the workplace and in housing. A year later he was shot and killed at City Hall, along with San Francisco mayor George Moscone, by disgruntled former supervisor Dan White.

Supervisor Harvey Milk was one of the United States' first openly gay politicians.

▶ Harvey Milk rides in the San Francisco Pride Parade on 25th June, 1978.

NOVEMBER
28
1660

BOYLE, MORAY AND WREN FORM THE ROYAL SOCIETY

Christopher Wren, Robert Boyle and Robert Moray were some of the most eminent thinkers in England and, after Wren had delivered a lecture at London's Gresham College, around a dozen men signed a declaration, committing themselves to promoting 'Physico-Mathematicall Experimentall Learning' – a college for the exploration of the natural world. The society received a royal charter in 1662 and later, under Sir Isaac Newton's leadership, became an important research arm of the British government. For more than three centuries it has been one of the most influential scientific organisations in the world, with the likes of Albert Einstein, Stephen Hawking and Charles Darwin all on its membership list.

A dozen men signed a declaration, committing themselves to promoting 'Physico-Mathematicall Experimentall Learning'.

NOVEMBER
29
1979

ST FRANCIS OF ASSISI IS NAMED THE PATRON SAINT OF ECOLOGISTS

St Francis of Assisi committed himself to a life of solitude and prayer after a number of visions. In one, he was in the ruined church of San Damiano outside Assisi when he heard the altar crucifix command him: 'Go, Francis, and repair my house, which, as you see, is well-nigh in ruins.' Despite the fact that he was a layperson, unlicensed to preach, Francis drew large crowds of followers, and eventually travelled to Rome to seek approval of his Franciscan order from Pope Innocent III – which he obtained in 1210. He tried to live his life like Jesus Christ, eschewing worldly goods and embracing poverty. He saw nature as being at one with God and was even said to preach to the birds and livestock. It was this love and respect for all creatures that resulted in his patronage of ecology and ecologists in 1979.

Francis committed himself to a life of solitude and prayer after a number of visions.

SHIRLEY CHISHOLM IS BORN

In 1968, Shirley Chisholm became the first black woman to serve in the United States Congress. Within three years, the former teacher and education consultant had set her sights on a bigger ticket: in 1972 she announced that she was running for the Democratic party's presidential nomination. She was the first woman to do so.

Though she only came fourth, in Congress she was a force to be reckoned with, speaking out against the Vietnam War, supporting the legalising of abortion, and hiring only women for her office. She was a founding member of the National Women's Political Caucus and the Congressional Black Caucus.

> **" I'm a revolutionary at heart, I've got to run, even though it might be the downfall of my career. "**
>
> SHIRLEY CHISHOLM

▼ Shirley Chisholm began life as a teacher but was later elected to Congress before being the first woman ever to stand to become US president.

CHAPTER

12

December

DECEMBER
1
1955

CIVIL RIGHTS ICON ROSA PARKS IS ARRESTED

Rosa Parks joined the Montgomery, Alabama, chapter of the NAACP in 1943. Her husband discouraged her – with segregation laws part of everyday life there, it was a dangerous place to be outspoken and black. Riding home from work on the bus, she was seated in the segregated black section when the driver asked her and three others to give up their seats for a white man (the whites-only section was full). While the other riders did as they were told, Parks did not.

▼ Rosa Parks seated towards the front of the bus in Montgomery, Alabama, in 1956.

Refusing to give up her seat led to her arrest. Parks later said:

> 66 **I wasn't tired physically, I was tired of giving in.** 99

The NAACP chapter president E. D. Dixon wanted to use Parks' case to argue in court against the segregation laws. She agreed, and after a year of appealing against her conviction through the courts, while a bus boycott by blacks drew attention to the cause in Montgomery, on 13th November, 1956, the Supreme Court ruled that bus segregation was unconstitutional.

NAPOLEON CROWNS HIMSELF EMPEROR OF FRANCE

When Napoleon Bonaparte took the Crown of Charlemagne from Pope Pius VII and placed it on his own head in Paris' Notre Dame Cathedral, he became the first French emperor in a thousand years, and a self-appointed one at that. The military strategist had risen through the ranks of the French Revolutionary Army, seizing control of the government to become first consul and dominate Europe. Now he was the head of his own vast empire. It would be ten years before he faced defeat at the hands of allied forces in 1814 and was exiled to the island of Elba.

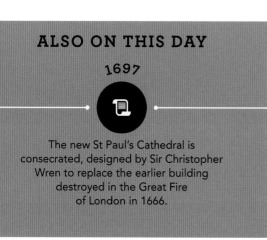

ALSO ON THIS DAY

1697

The new St Paul's Cathedral is consecrated, designed by Sir Christopher Wren to replace the earlier building destroyed in the Great Fire of London in 1666.

THE *NORTH STAR* IS FIRST PUBLISHED

Using funds from his public speaking tour of Great Britain and Ireland, American abolitionist Frederick Douglass put out the first edition of his anti-slavery newspaper in Rochester, New York. It would go on to become the most influential African-American publication of the pre-Civil War era. The paper included a forum for discrimination commentary, editorials, poetry, book reviews and letters from readers. The paper's name referred to the fact that those fleeing slavery used the North Star to navigate their way to freedom. Douglass became one of the country's most famous black men, fighting for equal rights – both for African-Americans and women – throughout the Civil War and beyond.

American abolitionist Frederick Douglass put out the first edition of his anti-slavery newspaper in Rochester, New York.

DECEMBER
4
1950

TONY BENN IS SWORN IN AS A MEMBER OF PARLIAMENT

Though never an official leader of Britain's Labour Party, Tony Benn was widely considered to be the leading voice of the radical leftist wing of the organisation. Although he came from a fairly wealthy background, Benn railed against the elite and the class system. He held cabinet posts as Secretary of State for Industry and then Energy. Benn believed in a different kind of economy: a democratic socialist system with open government and public ownership, expenditure and investment. After leaving Parliament, and in the wake of the September 11 attacks, he became president of the Stop the War Coalition, which he led until his death in 2014. He was a mentor to Jeremy Corbyn, who went on to win the Labour leadership contest a year after Benn's death.

> **Although he came from a fairly wealthy background, Benn railed against the elite and the class system.**

DECEMBER
5
63 BCE

ROMAN CONSUL CICERO READS THE LAST OF HIS *CATILINE ORATIONS*

The year he became consul, Cicero was 43, which made him the youngest man to reach such powerful heights without having come from a political Roman family. Cicero was one of the most prolific writers and powerful orators of his generation; he translated Greek philosophy into Latin, and his 900 surviving letters have helped historians understand ancient Rome in ways they could not otherwise have done. One of his defining moments in power was his suppression of the Catiline conspiracy, which planned to overthrow the Republic. His speeches on this subject, one of which was delivered on this day, were persuasive public rebukes of Senator Lucius Catilina who led the planned revolt.

ALSO ON THIS DAY

1492

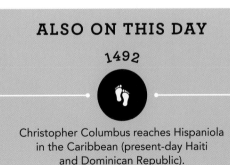

Christopher Columbus reaches Hispaniola in the Caribbean (present-day Haiti and Dominican Republic).

DECEMBER
6
1921

MICHAEL COLLINS SIGNS THE ANGLO-IRISH TREATY

Raised in Cork, Ireland, Michael Collins was from a proud nationalist farming family. Collins' father predicted on his deathbed that his son would do great things for the country. After being part of the failed Easter Rising in 1916, Collins was elected to the Sinn Féin executive and became commander of the Irish Republican Army. He was a respected leader, despite his involvement in deadly operations against the British, which was why he was sent to Westminster to help negotiate an Anglo-Irish treaty. Though the treaty ended the conflict, allowing 26 of the country's counties to become the Irish Free State, many people were unhappy with the partition and the fact that Ireland would not (as yet) become a republic. Collins' piggy-in-the-middle status ultimately led to his assassination in 1922.

▼ Michael Collins (second from left) with Arthur Griffith and members of the Irish delegation which negotiated the treaty.

DECEMBER

7

1916

LLOYD GEORGE REPLACES ASQUITH AS BRITISH PM

David Lloyd George had already made a name for himself as chancellor in Herbert Asquith's government, introducing state pensions for the first time in Britain and working to reduce poverty. But it was his wartime effort, first as munitions minister and then as prime minister, that saw him leave an indelible mark on British politics. He was called 'the man who won the war', and when the public, including some women for the first time, voted again in 1918, his coalition won a huge majority. By negotiating and signing the Treaty of Versailles a year later, he helped to establish the League of Nations. Domestically, he changed the future for Britain's children, raising the school leaving age to 14 and prohibiting the employment of school-age children.

It was Lloyd George's wartime effort that saw him leave an indelible mark on British politics.

DECEMBER

8

1980

PEACE ACTIVIST AND MUSICIAN LENNON IS ASSASSINATED

John Lennon rose to fame as one quarter of the Beatles, but after the band split, it was his activism, particularly in collaboration with his wife Yoko Ono, that kept him in the spotlight. The two artists worked together on a number of projects, the most famous of which were their two 1969 'Bed-ins for Peace'. Shortly after their highly publicised wedding, they invited the world's press to come and join them as they lay in bed in hotel rooms in Amsterdam and Montreal, promoting world peace while the war in Vietnam raged on.

Lennon rose to fame as one quarter of the Beatles, but after the band split, it was his activism that kept him in the spotlight.

Lennon was killed outside his New York apartment by Mark David Chapman, a former fan and born-again Christian who was angry with Lennon for saying the Beatles were "more popular than Jesus".

DECEMBER
9
1897

FEMINIST ACTIVIST MARGUERITE DURAND PUBLISHES *LA FRONDE*

La Fronde (*The Slingshot*) was a feminist newspaper for women, by women. Its title referred to a series of rebellions in France (1648–53) which attempted to rein in the powers of the monarchy; the working-class rebels were known for using slingshots to break windows. A British newspaper remarking on the publication commented that these feminist *frondeurs*

intend to fling stones with all their might at all those who oppose the march of the new woman.

Durand modelled *La Fronde* on popular dailies of the era. As well as feminist issues, it covered politics and the stock market.

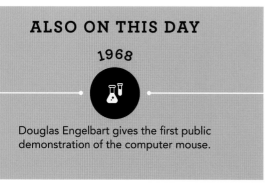

ALSO ON THIS DAY

1968

Douglas Engelbart gives the first public demonstration of the computer mouse.

DECEMBER
10
1931

NOBEL PEACE PRIZE IS AWARDED TO AN AMERICAN WOMAN

Jane Addams began her career as a reformer and activist by founding Hull House in Chicago. It was a 'settlement house' that brought together people from all social and economic groups, particularly immigrants. It was a centre for research, learning, culture, sports and community – a space where connections could be made and social services accessed. And through her work there, Addams came to be known as the 'Mother of Social Work' in America.

During World War I she travelled to The Hague, where she chaired the Women's Congress (an international gathering of women seeking to end the war and restore peace) and tried to encourage President Woodrow Wilson to mediate a peace agreement, rather than join the war. Though the peace negotiations in 1919 marginalised women's views and the importance of insisting on women's suffrage, out of the Congress came the Women's International League for Peace and Freedom, of which Addams was president, promoting peace and encouraging world powers to disarm in the wake of the war. It was for these efforts that she received the Nobel Peace Prize, making her the first American woman to receive the award and the second woman to have been given the award.

▲ Arrival of the American Mission in
Rotterdam on board SS *Noordam*.
Jane Addams is in the centre.

DECEMBER
11
1936

AFTER ABDICATING, EDWARD VIII ADDRESSES THE PUBLIC
The British Royal's love for the American divorcée Wallis Simpson led to his decision to end his reign.

DECEMBER
12
1951

PAULA ACKERMAN STARTS TO LEAD RABBINICAL SERVICES
After the death of her husband, Rabbi Dr. William Ackerman, Paula became the first woman in America to do so.

DECEMBER
13
1996

KOFI ANNAN IS ELECTED SECRETARY GENERAL When the Ghanaian diplomat was elected he became the first black African to lead the United Nations.

DECEMBER
14
1985

ACTIVIST WILMA MANKILLER TAKES OFFICE The first female principal chief of the Cherokee Nation oversaw the construction of new health clinics and education programmes.

DECEMBER
15
1890

SIOUX CHIEF AND HOLY MAN SITTING BULL IS KILLED After his surrender to the new settlers, he was killed during a shoot-out by government-paid Native American police officers.

DECEMBER
16
1916

RUSSIAN SPIRITUAL LEADER RASPUTIN IS ASSASSINATED
Rasputin's political power and sway over the royals resulted in his assassination. His body was found two days later.

DECEMBER
17
1907

WANGCHUCK BECOMES THE FIRST KING OF BHUTAN
Though the pious Buddhist and military leader established the monarchy in 1907, he had already ruled for ten years.

DECEMBER
18
1865

THE 13TH AMENDMENT IS ADDED TO THE US CONSTITUTION

It was 246 years since the first captive Africans disembarked at Jamestown, Virginia, and were sold, marking the start of the slave trade in America. As the Civil War was winding down and with victory in sight, President Abraham Lincoln's Republican Party introduced the 13th amendment, concerned that the Emancipation Proclamation, issued two years earlier, needed to be cemented in the constitution. A couple of weeks earlier, Alabama had become the 27th state to ratify the amendment, giving it the three-quarters majority it needed to become law. The Amendment ensured that

neither slavery nor involuntary servitude ... shall exist within the United States, or any place subject to their jurisdiction.

DECEMBER

19

1675

METACOMET'S NATION SUFFERS IN THE GREAT SWAMP MASSACRE

Chief Metacomet took the name King Philip in recognition of his Wampanoag people's harmonious relationship with the North American colonists. But, as the white settlers encroached more on Wampanoag lands and his people faced humiliation and harsh punishment, Metacomet feared they would lose all right to their land if nothing was done. This resulted in a three-year conflict known as King Philip's War. Metacomet led a tribal coalition against the ill-trained militia, destroying settlements in Connecticut and Massachusetts. This critical battle, which took place in present-day Rhode Island, was an attack on the Narragansett tribe, who had attempted to remain neutral in the conflict and were sheltering wanted Wampanoag people. Approximately 600 Native Americans lost their lives in the Great Swamp when the soldiers burned the Narragansett encampment.

> **Approximately 600 Native Americans lost their lives in the Great Swamp.**

DECEMBER

20

69 CE

THE ROMAN SENATE RECOGNISES EMPEROR VESPASIANUS

Titus Vespasianus was the fourth Roman leader in the Year of the Four Emperors, a period of civil war that saw leadership change hands as rivals clamoured for power in the wake of Nero's death. Vespasian was a trusted aide of Nero's, and governor of Africa. His support among the legions there helped him defeat previous claimants to the top job: Galba, Otho and then Vitellius. Once victorious, he sent his commander, Primus, to Italy, where the Senate passed a law proclaiming Vespasian emperor. During his 27-year reign, the first of the Flavian dynasty, he rebuilt Rome's coffers (depleted by Nero's recklessness), restored discipline to the empire's armies and ushered in a period of stability for the people.

ALSO ON THIS DAY

1192

King Richard I 'the Lionheart' of England is imprisoned by Duke Leopold V of Austria, whom he had offended at the siege of Acre during the Third Crusade.

DECEMBER

21

1958

FREE FRENCH LEADER CHARLES DE GAULLE IS ELECTED FIRST PRESIDENT OF THE FIFTH REPUBLIC

France's World War II hero, Charles De Gaulle, had received a celebratory welcome when he arrived in Paris in 1944 and had gone on to be the provisional president of the country. But, after limited electoral success in the years that followed, he had left politics in 1953. Then a revolt in Algeria by French colonists developed into a political crisis. With the Fourth Republic destroyed, De Gaulle returned to the political arena to lead his country again, with emergency powers to rule by decree for six months. A new constitution, shaped by De Gaulle, was approved in September, and the nationalistic leader was voted into power a couple of months later. He then set about strengthening France, both financially and militarily.

> **A revolt in Algeria by French colonists developed into a political crisis.**

▼ Charles de Gaulle (centre) arrives in Paris, France, to celebrate the liberation of the city.

DECEMBER

22

1944

AMERICAN GENERAL ANTHONY MCAULIFFE REFUSES TO SURRENDER AT THE BATTLE OF THE BULGE

It was the Germans' last major offensive of the war, and the largest World War II battle in which the United States fought, but American General Anthony McAuliffe, who was commanding the 101st Airborne Division when the Germans attempted to push the Allied front line west into northwestern Belgium, was not in a surrendering kind of mood. The massive German offensive had taken the Allies by surprise, and McAuliffe's men were holed up in Bastogne, surrounded by German armoured divisions. Things were looking pretty grim, but when German forces sent an ultimatum, demanding their 'honourable surrender', the American general sent a missive back saying:

"To the German Commander:
NUTS!
The American Commander"

The Americans waited for reinforcements instead, and after several more weeks, with thousands of casualties on both sides, the Allies had retaken their lost territory and were heading towards Berlin.

▲ Lieutenant General George S. Patton (centre) talks with Brigadier General Anthony McAuliffe in Bastogne, France, on 28th December, 1944.

DECEMBER
23
1745

AMERICAN FOUNDING FATHER JOHN JAY IS BORN

Born into a wealthy New York merchant family, John Jay was drawn to the law and later politics, being elected to the first Continental Congress, where delegates debated the oppressive laws of British colonial rule. During the Revolutionary War he put his diplomacy skills to work in Spain, drumming up financial backing for the conflict. He was also one of the five-member peace commission that negotiated the Treaty of Paris to end the war, pressing for British recognition of American independence. George Washington appointed him as the first chief justice of the United States – the country's highest judicial position – and he later served as governor of New York, where he fought for the abolition of slavery in the state.

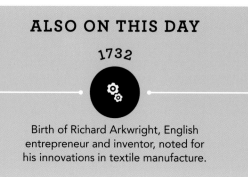

ALSO ON THIS DAY

1732

Birth of Richard Arkwright, English entrepreneur and inventor, noted for his innovations in textile manufacture.

DECEMBER
24
1166

ELEANOR OF AQUITAINE GIVES BIRTH TO KING JOHN OF ENGLAND

Eleanor of Aquitaine spent nearly 70 years as one of the most powerful women in medieval Europe, married two kings and gave birth to three more. She was the eldest daughter of William X, Duke of Aquitaine, a powerful landowner who ruled over more of France than the king. She inherited his impressive fortune and at 15 was married to the future King Louis VII. When the marriage broke down 15 years later, she had it annulled, and all of her private property was returned to her. She then set her sights on Henry Plantagenet, the future king of England. By marrying and combining her lands with his, they forged a vast empire, and cemented it through the strategic marriages of their children. They travelled widely, wanting the people of their cross-cultural empire to see them as active rulers – this meant that Eleanor played a prominent role in governing their domain, something she continued to do after her husband's death, when her sons were on the throne.

Eleanor married two kings and gave birth to three more.

DECEMBER

25

1066

WILLIAM THE CONQUEROR BECOMES KING OF ENGLAND

Known as William the Great by his admirers (the 'Conqueror' name appeared in the 1120s), he led the Norman Conquest that changed the face of Britain. After King Harold II's death at the Battle of Hastings in 1066, William marched to London, which submitted. Then on Christmas Day that year, at Westminster Abbey, he became the first Norman king of England.

Although he made some positive changes in Britain, such as banning the slave trade, building great stone churches and castles, and creating the Domesday Book, a survey of England and Wales and their people, William was one of the most brutal leaders in European history (by his own admission), whose rule was resented and resisted by the Saxons for years after the Conquest.

▼ William the Conqueror (centre) defeats the English army at the Battle of Hastings.

DECEMBER

26

1943

ADMIRAL SIR BRUCE FRASER SINKS THE GERMAN BATTLE CRUISER *SCHARNHORST*

After this torpedo victory off the north Norwegian coast, the Admiralty signalled 'Grand. Well Done,' to the fleet's commander. *Scharnhorst* had posed a critical naval threat to the Allied forces and to a key supply line to Russia.

In the critical years 1939 to 1942, Sir Bruce Fraser was responsible for the Royal Navy's expansion, and then in 1943 he took on the role of commander in chief of the Home Fleet, protecting Russian convoys delivering much-needed supplies. These convoys tied up Germany's air and naval forces and proved the Allies' commitment to the Soviet Union. Fraser went on to command the British Pacific Fleet, which was vital to the defeat of Japanese forces and the end of World War II. After the war, Fraser was given the title Lord Fraser of North Cape.

▼ *Scharnhorst*, the flagship of the German East Asia Squadron, is charging in the port of Valparaiso, Chile.

DECEMBER
27
2007

FORMER PAKISTANI PM BHUTTO IS ASSASSINATED

Benazir Bhutto was the first woman to lead a democratic government in a Muslim-majority nation, coming to power in 1988 after transforming the Pakistan People's Party. The controversial leader served two terms but was later charged with corruption. She had narrowly survived an assassination attempt a few months earlier, when she arrived in Karachi to begin her re-election campaign after spending eight years abroad in self-imposed exile. But in December she was not so lucky. While campaigning in Rawalpindi, she was waving to the crowds through the sunroof of her armoured vehicle when she was shot at. A suicide bomb went off seconds later, killing her.

ALSO ON THIS DAY

1831

British naturalist Charles Darwin embarks on his five-year voyage of exploration aboard HMS *Beagle*.

DECEMBER
28
1860

SEWARD ACCEPTS LINCOLN'S OFFER TO BE SECRETARY OF STATE

William Seward had been hoping to be president himself, but it was Abraham Lincoln who changed the course of history when he won the presidency on 6th November. Seward was not on the ballot, having lost out at the Republican Convention, despite being the favourite to earn the nomination. As Seward was the party's leading figure, and had campaigned actively for Lincoln's election, it was convention for the new president to offer him the important cabinet position of secretary of state, but Seward took his time before replying. The two men would go on to have an effective working relationship, with Seward becoming one of Lincoln's closest advisors, helping him to navigate the precarious Civil War years. He continued to serve as Secretary of State under President Andrew Johnson, after Lincoln's assassination, and in 1867 he negotiated the purchase of Alaska from Russia.

> Seward had been hoping to be president himself, but it was Lincoln who changed the course of history.

DECEMBER

29

1170

THOMAS BECKET IS ASSASSINATED

Thomas Becket was the chancellor of England, one of the highest official positions in Henry II's court. All official documents passed under his nose, and as a close confidant and advisor to the king he wielded considerable power. When the archbishop of Canterbury died, Henry appointed Becket to the post, despite the fact that he was not a priest, in order to have a tighter grip on both Church and state. But Becket saw the position as a religious calling, taking the role seriously and living the simple life of a monk, preferring to uphold the position of the Church rather than use the institution to do Henry's bidding. With neither man backing down, Becket risked his life, which was eventually taken from him by a group of assassins, most likely on the king's orders. They found him in Canterbury Cathedral, where they attacked him with swords. After his death, Becket became a martyr and his place of burial a pilgrimage site.

▼ Thomas Becket, English churchman, saint and martyr, pleads with his assassins.

DECEMBER
30
1906

SOCIAL REFORMER JOSEPHINE BUTLER DIES

Josephine Butler played a pivotal role in changing the education and public health landscape in Britain, particularly for women. She had been raised by a social reformer and abolitionist, and got involved in charity work after the death of her daughter. She was concerned with the rights of women and teenage sex workers, campaigning successfully for the age of consent to be raised from 13 to 16, and put pressure on Cambridge University to offer higher education to women. But she is best known for her opposition to the Contagious Diseases Acts, which placed the blame for venereal disease on women and gave the police powers to force intimate examinations on women they believed to be sex workers.

DECEMBER
31
1972

AMERICAN GAY RIGHTS PIONEER HENRY GERBER DIES

Known as the 'Grandfather of the American Gay Rights Movement', Henry Gerber died at the age of 80 after dedicating much of his life to the fight for civil rights for gay people. Born in Bavaria, he immigrated to the United States in 1913 before spending three years in the US Army, stationed in occupied Germany, after World War I. Inspired by the gay rights movements gathering momentum there, on his return to the United States he started the Chicago Society for Human Rights, facing much resistance. It is believed to have been America's first gay rights organisation. Gerber suffered arrest and prosecution for his advocacy efforts.

ALSO ON THIS DAY

1892

The physician Dr Miles V. Lynk publishes the first black medical journal.

ALSO ON THIS DAY

1879

US inventor Thomas Alva Edison demonstrates the incandescent light bulb.

INDEX

CREDITS

The publisher would like to thank the following for the permission to reproduce copyright material:

Alamy
Painting by Charles Joseph Natoire/ Peter Horree: p19; johnrochaphoto/ China: p23; Granger Historical Picture Archive: p55; Chronicle: p63 ; 506 collection: p64; Pictorial Press Ltd: p71; Keystone Pictures USA: p73; Lakeview Images: p76; Pictorial Press Ltd: p123; Chronicle: p124; Science History Images: p143; The History Collection: p184; Robert Clay: p197.

Getty Images
Keystone/Stringer/Getty: p7; Hulton Archive: p11; Ean-Claude Francolon/ Gamma-Rapho: p14; Keystone/Hulton Archive: p16; Prisma/UIG: p27; Universal History Archive/ UIG: p31; Chuck Kennedy/MCT: p33; MPI/ Stringer: p37; Popperfoto: p38; Gallo Images/Business Day/Robert Botha: p41; The Print Collector: p43; Bettmann: p46; TASS: p49; Keystone-France/Gamma-Keyston: p50; Marie Hansen/The LIFE Picture Collection: p53; Corbis: p56; American Photo Archive: p58; Popperfoto: p59; AFP: p62; Brendan Smialowski-Pool: p79; AFP: p82; Keystone / Stringer: p87 Terence Spencer/The LIFE Images Collection: p91; MPI / Stringer: p96; Keystone: p98; Bill Eppridge/The LIFE Picture Collection: p99; Boris Spremo: p111; Historical: p127; DEA / Biblioteca Ambrosiana: p130; Print Collector: p138; Guildhall Library & Art Gallery/ Heritage Images: p140; Anwar Hussein: p145; MPI/ Stringer: p147; Apic: p148; Print Collector: p152; FILES/J. David AKE/AFP: p155; Keystone/ Stringer: p157; Alfred Eisenstaedt: p161; PhotoQuest: p165; Culture club: p166; Photo 12: p168; AFP: p175; PhotoQuest: p176; Bettmann: p179; Bettmann: 181; UIG: p187; Ed Vebell: p191; Bettmann: p201; Topical Press Agency: p204; Bettmann: p207; Popperfoto: p210; PhotoQuest: p211; Popperfoto: p213; Popperfoto: p216.

Shutterstock
Stockphotocorner: p66; Everett Historical: p77; Everett Historical: p95; Nigel Jarvis: p162; Everett Historical: p188; Photocosmos: p193; Bodini/ AP: p195.

Other
LSE Library/ Flickr: p104; Creative commons: p108, p169, p172, p214; NASA: p119, p214; Library of Congress/Roger Higgins: p199; NASA: p119; Public domain: p101, p114, p129, p134, p183.

While every effort has been made to credit photographers and artists, The Bright Press would like to apologise should there be any omissions or errors and would be pleased to make appropriate corrections for future editions of the book.

ACKNOWLEDGEMENTS

This book has been a thrilling historical exploration and a lesson in fantastic and fearsome leadership. Putting it together required a few of those skills great leaders know only too well: project management, strategic thinking and copious amounts of tea-drinking. (It's probably true that all great leaders are caffeinated to the max.) In general, though, I'm more of a follower. I follow my amazing husband when we go running, trailing behind like a lazy corgi, and I willingly follow my wonderful friends to the pub and my awesome professional peers on Twitter. While this book would definitely have been possible without them, it wouldn't have been written by such a lucky lady. And lastly, I'd like to dedicate this book to my wonderful family – I would follow you all anywhere, even Jameils, as long as there's cake.